THE PEARLS OF THE GULF

NAPLES
CAPRI · SORRENTO

ISCHIA · POZZUOLI · SOLFATARA · BAIA · CUMAE

BACOLI – CAPO MISENO · ISLAND OF PROCIDA · MASSA LUBRENSE
SANT'AGATA SUI DUE GOLFI · CASTELLAMMARE DI STABIA

BONECHI

© Copyright   by Casa Editrice Bonechi, via Cairoli 18/b - Florence - Italy
Tel (55)576841 - Telex 571323 CEB - Fax (55)5000766
Printed in Italy by Centro Stampa Editoriale Bonechi.
The cover, layout and artwork by the Casa Editrice Bonechi graphic artists in this publication are protected by international copyright.
Text and Editing: Giuliano Valdes, Editing Studio - Pisa
English translation: Rhiannon Lewis
Type-setting: Linotipia Colombo snc - Bolzano
Plates: La Fotolitografia - Florence
The photographs are the property of the Archives of Casa Editrice Bonechi.
Photo Barone: pages 4, 5, 13, 34, 37, 42a, 52, 87-97.
Photo Tripodi: pages 1, 36.

ISBN 88-7009-713-7

* * *

INTRODUCTION

The mere mention of the words "Gulf of Naples" immediately conjours up a kaleidoscope of brilliant pictures; varied, vivid, well-defined and often contrasting, but all having in common a wide and profoundly intense involvement of the senses, usually mixed with high-flown sentiments. The natural surroundings of this area, which for thousands of years have borne the indelible stamp of the presence of man, reveal primordial aspects which arouse feelings of amazement and marvel interspersed with anxiety and solicitude. If on the one hand the unparalleled stimulation gained from the Mediterranean environment has always aroused wonder in tourists from all over the world, on the other hand the vulcanic nature of the Parthenopean gulf, the instability of the terrafirma in the large southern metropolis, the disturbing questions raised by the Flegrean region - not to mention "himself", the sombre lord of the gulf who, under the guise of a serene and peaceful mountain rules over the fortunes of a much wider territory which is heavily populated - cannot do other than induce us to reflect on how many people are involved in safeguarding and preserving one of the more beautiful corners of this wonderful country.

The classical authors of the Latinity called it "Campania Felix"; "lucky" Campania, from time immemorial, because of the extraordinary fertility of its vulcanic soil, the unrivaled mildness of its gentle Mediterranean climate and the unique splendour of its extremely rich and varied countryside. In this ancient and singular region Naples and its gulf play a primary role. Less than 39 kms separate Mount Cuma, on the most westerly point of the Flegrean Fields, from Punta Campanella, situated on the end of the Sorrento peninsula. Along this perfect arc are to be found the pearls of the picturesque and evocative Parthenopean "necklace": the Flegrean Islands - Ischia, Procida and Vivara - Bacoli, Miseno, Baia, Cuma, Pozzuoli and the Solfatara crater, Naples and Vesuvius, Castellammare di Stabia, Sorrento and its coast and Capri.

This fan-shaped area, which is itself a rich and exhaustive source of propositions, acts as a starting point for other tourist itineraries and destinations, which each visitor can adapt to his own needs and specific interests. The Gulf of Naples district contains an exceptional amount of art and historical works, besides a superlative open-air nature museum. Evidence of man's evolution - from the beginning of the Roman era, through the Dark Ages, up to the troubled present times, ending with the contradictions and unsolved problems of contemporary society - is forceably placed in the natural surroundings which act as a backdrop to the remains of the past and to the bold and futuristic architectural solutions which have been brought to completion during the past few decades.

Those who wish to understand the real nature of Naples and its numerous tourist sites must necessarily look beyond certain obsolete and outworn stereotypes such as the sun, the pizza, the spaghetti and the tarantella. Even if the Parthenopean gulf region is without a shadow of doubt among the sunnier spots in the Mediterranean, even if its sea and its sky are among the bluer and more serene in Italy, even if the splendour of its coast and the lush vegetation gratify the senses of the visitor, it is however necessary to investigate its cultural aspects. These go deeper than its treasures in art, history, architecture and craftsmanship, even though these take a major role, and descend into the realms of folk-lore and popular traditions; into that genuine and outspoken culture which invented the pizza and the Neapolitan song but which has always had its own indomitable identity, in spite of the various dominating powers. The art of making-do and picking up the pieces to start out afresh, the ancestral desire to infringe the rules and mix the sacred with the profane - like the blood of San Gennaro (St. Januarius) and the lottery numbers, the pyrotechnical and liberating joie de vivre, Piedigrotta or the successes of the local football team - have become part of a custom which cannot be denied.

NAPLES

Splendidly situated overlooking the picturesque gulf which is bounded by Capo Miseno and Punta Campanella, the city is laid out in a semicircle, between the vulcanic amphitheatres of the Flegrean Fields and Vesuvius. Naples is the main southern metropolis as regards urban dimensions, the third largest Italian city by demographic size and one of the major Mediterranean calling-ports as well as a naval and strategic base. Prominent magnetic pole for a wide belt of the Campania region and for the internal regions, it is a vital communications junction for road, rail and sea traffic and is served by an airport which is the third in importance after those of Rome and Milan. Its economic structure is founded on the growth of industrial, commercial and general services sectors which still present disharmony and structural imbalance that reflect heavily on the social structure, where the contrast between the thriving wealthy districts and the vast pockets of need and poverty, aggravated by the carelessness and urbanistic degradation of some central and suburban districts, are all too obvious. Among other things the huge proliferation of the urban web has actually caused the merging with some of the large important nearby centres, so that the area covered by Naples has grown out of all proportion over the last few decades.

The site now occupied by the city was first colonized by settlers from Rhodes and was known as *Parthenope*. It was later known as *Paleopolis* (the "old city") and received a substantial impetus as a consequence of the foundation of the colony of Cumae (9th century B.C.). The original nucleus of the city, founded on the site now occupied by the dell'Ovo Castle, was joined around the 5th century B.C. by *Neapolis* (the "new city") founded by Greek settlers who came from Euboea. At the time when the Siracusan expansion was at its peak it grew in importance, establishing itself as the principle city in the region, partly thanks to the contribution given by the inhabitants of Cumae who had fled after the Samnite conquest. In the second half of the 4th century B.C. Neapolis was drawn into the sphere of Roman influence, becoming an ally of the powerful neighbouring city in the wars which the latter fought against the Carthaginians for the control of the Mediterranean basin. After becoming a *municipium* (90 B.C.), and badly scarred by the civil war (82 B.C.), the city nonetheless conserved the cultural prerogatives of its

Mergellina, a picturesque view of the seaside village.

*Panorama of Naples: old and modern are mingled
under the unmistakable outline of Vesuvius.*

Greek origin and the attractions offered by its countryside and climate which perpetuated, even during the Imperial era, the tendency of the Roman nobility and patriarchs to settle here, erecting sumptuous residences and splendid villas. The spread of Christianity brought persecutions to Naples; the most illustrious victim was Gennaro (Januarius), Bishop of Benevento, who suffered martyrdom at Pozzuoli (4th century) and who has since been venerated as the patron saint of the city. The breaking up of the Roman Empire brought the conquest by the Goths (5th century) who were followed by the Byzantines. From the second half of the 8th century it became a self-contained duchy, managing to conserve its independence, with the exception of a brief Longobard period, holding out against repeated bids for its conquest by the Moslems. The Norman conquest under Roger d'Altavilla (1139) started the downward trend of Naples' predominance which before long found itself stripped of its title of capital city in favour of Palermo. After the constitution of the Free Commune which came about under papal auspices (1251), it saw the Swabian decadence and the arrival of the Angevins who reinstated it as the capital. The Angevin period brought about an urban revival and marked a new development in the cultural life. Under Aragonese rule the city took part in the dispute between the Spanish and the French which was concluded with the succession to the throne of Charles VIII (at the end of the 15th century). The subsequent Spanish rule which continued until the end of the 18th century is one of the most troublesome pages in the history of Naples, marked by frequent uprisings by the population (that of Masaniello in 1647 is famous) and tormented by epidemics of the plague. Taken by the Austrians and consigned to Charles of Bourbon, Naples regained its former splendour as the capital of an autonomous kingdom (1734). In the wake of Transalpine events the city experimented with the shortlived Neapolitan Republic. After the reigns of Giuseppe Bonaparte and Murat it returned under the Bourbons who made it the capital of the Kingdom of Sicily. In the meantime the Renaissance unrest paved the way for the first uprisings (1820, 1848) which laid the foundations for Garibaldi's victorious undertaking and for the annexation to Piedmont (1860). During the last war it was sorely tested, managing to free itself from the nazi oppression during the epic Quattro Giornate in September 1943. On November 23rd 1980 Naples was hit by the disastrous earthquake which shook the Irpinia and Basilicata regions and which caused 56 deaths in the city.

5

PIAZZA DEL MUNICIPIO
(TOWN HALL SQUARE)

The central Town Hall Square is one of the focal points of the feverish Neapolitan traffic and extends, sloping almost imperceptively downwards and overlooked by the characteristic outline of Vesuvius, between the Palace of the same name and the *Stazione Marittima* (Harbour Station) which is built in the unmistakeable style of the late 1930's and delimits the built-up district towards the marina. The tree-lined square has many plants and fountains and is placed in an urban setting which is characterised by buildings that often contrast each other by date and architectural style. At the top of the square towards the hillside rises the massive structure of *St. Elmo's Castle* dominating the *Carthusian Monastery of St. Martin*, which lies below it. Important commercial streets, such as the *Via Medina, Via Depretis* and *Via St. Carlo* which make up the cornerstone of the services sector in this city, branch off at the sides of the square. The 19th-century **Town Hall** which was once the seat of the Bourbon Government is flanked by the **Church of S. Giacomo degli Spagnoli** which was erected around the middle of the 16th century by Don Pedro di Toledo, viceroy of Spain. Towering over the square on a high pedestal facing the statue of *Partenope* is the equestrian monument to *Victor Emmanuel II.*

Two prospects of the Town Hall Square towered over by the statue of Victor Emanuel II.

View of the Angevin Fortress.

MASCHIO ANGIOINO
(ANGEVIN FORTRESS)

The characteristic outline of this huge fortress stands out clearly on the water-front between Santa Lucia and the Stazione Marittima (Harbour Station), acting as a focal point for arrivals from the sea. Also known as *Castel Nuovo* (the New Castle) from the time of its construction, probably in order to distinguish it from already existing fortresses in the city, it has a singular shape, being built on an irregular four-sided plan with battlemented walls rising from a scarp foundation and reinforced by robust circular corner towers crowned by merlons and brackets. It was constructed in the second half of the 13th century by Pietro de Caulis for Charles I of Anjou (from which it derives its name *Maschio Angioino*). Almost two centuries later Alphonse I of Aragon arranged for substantial renovations to be carried out and it was almost completely rebuilt. The works which took place at the beginning of the 15th century were placed in the hands of Tuscan and Catalan master craftsmen who left the marks of their individual architectural concepts.

One of the most valuable features of the building in terms of architecture, style and art, dates back to that era (1455 - 1468): the **Arco di Trionfo** (Triumphal Arch). This is without doubt one of the most conspicuous contributions to Renaissance honorary architecture, since it is a fusion of the art of the major representatives of sculpture at that time with the traditional canons of Roman commemorative arches, on which it was clearly inspired. The arch stands between the *Torre di Mezzo* (Central Tower) and the *Torre di Guardia* (Watchtower), making a contrast between the whiteness of its lines and the darker piperno (a type of trachyte frequently used in Naples for building material). It was erected to commemorate the entry into Naples of Alphonse I of Aragon (26 of February 1443) and has a complex structure consisting of an arch flanked

7

Angevin Fortress: two details of the Triumphal Arch can be admired on the next page.

by Corinthian columns set side by side (in the interior curve are several basreliefs representing *Alphonse among his family and dignitaries*) and has an Attic bearing a frieze representing *The Triumphal Entry of Alphonse I*. Over the Attic there is another arch between pairs of Ionic columns holding up a second Attic decorated with niches in which there are statues of *Temperance, Strength, Justice and Magnanimity*. Crowning this magnificent work is a semi-circular panel with the allegorical representation of *Two Rivers* presided over by the *Archangel Michael*. Among the important sculptors who worked on this cycle were Francesco Laurana, Domenico Gagini, Isaia da Pisa and Pére Johan.

The castle was the residence of the Angevin and Aragonese courts and was both witness to and participant in the animated story of this city. Among its illustrious visitors were Pope Celestino V, Giotto, Petrarch, Boccaccio, Antonio Beccadelli (known as il Panormita), T. Caracciolo, G. Pontano and D. Carafa, Ettore Fieramosca, Charles V. During the 16th to 18th centuries it was renovated and modified several times and was restored to its original 15th-century aspect by restoration work carried out at the beginning of this century. Its numerous interiors include the *Courtyard* which has an interesting 16th - century portal; the *Church of St. Barbara*, also known as the *Palatine Chapel* or *Church of St. Sebastian*, one of the few original buildings to reach our times, and which has an interesting sculpture by Laurana and Andrea dell'Aquila and traces of frescoes by Maso di Banco; the *Sala dei Baroni* (Baronial Hall) which contains works by Laurana and Domenico Gagini (partly ruined by fire).

Trieste e Trento Square: Vista of the Church of St. Ferdinand with King Umberto I's Arcade in the background.

Some views of the central King Umberto I's Arcade. ►

GALLERIA UMBERTO I
(KING UMBERTO I'S ARCADE)

Piazza Trieste e Trento (Trieste and Trento Square), enriched by a rather modern fountain, is to be found in the heart of the old town a short distance from the *Piazza del Plebiscito* (The Square of the Plebiscite). Facing onto the square is the **Church of St. Ferdinand** with its characteristic frontal on two orders which was built in the 17th century to plans drawn up by Conforto and elaborated on during the same century by Fanzago. It was originally a place of worship for the Jesuits and for a long time it acted as the headquarters of the *Archiconfraternity of our Lady of the Seven Sorrows)*. The façade which has vertical pilaster strips on two orders, has a series of lovely niches on the bottom order and a portal flanked by columns supporting a frieze decorated with sculptures. On the pinnacle of the edifice there is a triangular timpano with a central coat of arms. The single-naved interior houses sculptures by Vaccaro and frescoes carried out by Paolo de Matteis. Leaving the square by *Via St. Carlo* brings one to **King Umberto I's Arcade** which is entered through an elegant neoclassic front, decorated with numerous columns and sculptures. The typically Umbertine construction was completed between the end of the last century and the beginning of this one and is interesting for its daring iron and glass structure which culminates in a high dome resting on an octagonal base. The elaborately decorated arcade was designed by E. Rocco, P. Boubée, A. Curri and E. di Mauro and is one of the places favoured by the Neapolitans for meeting friends and for the evening stroll. In front of the main entrance to the arcade is the **Theatre of S. Carlo** which is one of the major temples of Italian opera, and in fact of world-wide importance, and is noted for the elegance of its spacious interior. Built in the first half of the 18th century on the instructions of Charles of Bourbon, it was further improved on by Bibiena and Fuga. At the beginning of the last century the atrium and the loggia on the façade were added and the interior, which had been destroyed by fire, was reconstructed by the architect Niccolini.

The Square of the Plebiscite: The façade of the Royal Palace.

Some of the interiors of the Royal Palace. ▶

PALAZZO REALE
(ROYAL PALACE)

This huge monumental construction dominates the central *Piazza del Plebiscito* (the Square of the Plebiscite) which can be considered one of the most interesting squares in Naples because of its artistic and architectural merits. The drawing up of a project for the construction of a royal palace in Naples was presided over by Domenico Fontana who began work at the beginning of the 17th century. The Spanish viceroy Don Ferrante Ruiz de Castro, who wished to erect a residence worthy of his king, Philip II, on the ocassion of his visit to the city, was patron of this colossal undertaking.

The building as it is seen by today's tourists owes its aspect to a series of transformations, modifications and restructurations over the course of the centuries which have left only the façade and the main courtyard in their original state. At the beginning of the 18th century it was restructured and enlarged and was then repristined by Gaetano Genovese who made substantial neoclassical changes to the building after it had been destroyed by a fire at the time of Ferdinand II (1837).

The dramatic façade which is crowned by a clock with a small belfry alligns two heavy orders of windows alternated by pilaster strips. On the ground floor the ancient orig-inal portal was partly modified by Vanvitelli who made several niches populated by statues representing the following, from left to right: *Roger the Norman, Frederich II of Swabia, Charles I of Anjou, Alphonse I of Aragon, Charles V, Charles III of Bourbon, Gioacchino Murat, Victor Emmanuel II.* In the courtyard, near the beautiful 17th-century staircase which is the work of Picchiatti and was restructured by Genovese, there is a bronze door brought here from the Angevin Fortress. It is a very precious work of art and was carried out by Guglielmo Monaco and Pietro di Martino.

The **Teatro di Corte** (Court Theatre), built by Fuga in the second half of the 18th century is worth a visit; the **Central, Throne and Hercules' Halls** together with numerous other rooms form a museum which is rich in interesting period furnishings, porcelain, tapestries, Gobelins and paintings from the 17th - 18th centuries mostly carried out by local artists. The 17th-century **Chapel** which was brought to completion by Genovese is also worthy of note. The palace is furthermore site of the **Biblioteca Nazionale** (National Library) which conserves the famous papyri found at Herculaneum.

The Square of the Plebiscite: The Basilica of St. Francis of Paola.

Giovanni Bovio Square: two views of the lovely ► Neptune's Fountain.

BASILICA OF ST. FRANCIS OF PAOLA

The classical lines of the Basilica tower over the Doric columns which frame the monumental *Piazza del Plebiscito* (the Square of the Plebiscite), with its bronze equestrian statues of *Charles III of Bourbon* (A. Canova) and *Ferdinand I* (A. Calì). The present square was the result of the transformation, at the time of Gioacchino Murat, of an area near the Royal Palace. Leopoldo Laperuta was the instigator of the imposing colonnade which gives the square its lovely semicircular shape.

The Basilica of St. Francis of Paola, which is modelled along the lines of the Pantheon at Rome, was built at the beginning of the 19th century by the architect Pietro Bianchi. The central dome which is supported on a high tambour is flanked by two minor domes. The pronaos on the façade culminates in a triangular panel on which stand the statues representing *Religion, St. Ferdinand of Castile* and *St. Francis of Paola*. The interior has a circular form and conserves a valuable high altar in which many semiprecious stones have been used, and numerous sculptures and paintings.

PIAZZA GIOVANNI BOVIO (GIOVANNI BOVIO SQUARE)

The square is situated at the busy crossroads where *Via Depretis, Via Sanfelice and Corso Umberto I* (known locally as "Rettifilo") converge, carrying the bustling Neapolitan traffic. At the centre of the square the 17th-century **Fontana del Nettuno** (Neptune's Fountain), surrounded by an elegant wrought-iron railing, is shown to good advantage. The work is believed to be by Domenico Fontana. The figure of *Neptune* was carried out by Michelangelo Naccherino, while the *Sea Monsters* are the work of Piero Bernini. The fountain's present position dates from the end of the last century. Of particular interest are the *lions* and the *coats of arms* which decorate the balustrade and which are the result of Cosimo Fanzago's additions to the original fountain.

Elegant buildings face onto the square, among which the 19th-century **Palazzo della Borsa** (Stock Exchange) designed by A. Guerra. Next to the entrance staircase are two bronzes by Luigi de Luca representing *Genius dominating Strength*. The ancient **Chapel of St. Aspreno al Porto** (8th century) is situated on the spot where there were once Roman baths and was completely altered in the 17th century.

THE COASTAL AREA

The sunny Mediterranean atmosphere of Naples is enhanced by its luminous sea-front, by the wide roads, and by the district which faces onto the picturesque harbour. Next to *Port Sannazaro*, near the tunnel which runs through the Piedigrotta hill, is **Sannazaro Square** with its gardens, palm trees and lovely *Fountain*. The group of sculptures represents a *Mermaid with Dolphins and Seahorses*. At the end of Via Partenope, the elegant sea-front road lined with beautiful buildings and luxury-class hotels leads to **Borgo Marinaro** and the picturesque *Santa Lucia harbour*. This corner of the Neapolitan sea-front, which is extolled by a lovely well-known popular song and is known for some of the best restaurants in the city, is nowadays a harbour for small boats, while the fishermen continue to ply their centuries-old task in its idyllic setting. The view of Via Partenope is completed by the beautiful **Fontana dell'Immacolatella** (Fountain of the Young Virgin), which frames Mount Vesuvius in its marble arches. The 17th-century fountain is decorated with caryatids by Naccherino and sculptures by Bernini.

Sannazaro Square: the Siren's Fountain.

Via Partenope.

A view of Borgo Marinaro with the picturesque ►
harbour St. Lucia.

The elegant Fountain of the Yourg Virgin. ►

Some pictures of the dell'Ovo Castle at the end of the prospect from Via Caracciolo.

On the following pages: two angles of the Baroque Virgin Mary's Spire

CASTEL DELL'OVO
(DELL'OVO CASTLE)

This beautiful castle surrounded by water is one of the most characteristic sights on the Parthenopean waterfront. Its massive presence at the end of the Santa Lucia prominence can be seen from afar from the wide harbour roads and particularly from *Via Caracciolo* whose gently curving lines join the Via Partenope and Borgo Marinaro to the charming *Mergellina* harbour. The Via Partenope is fronted for a long tract by the **Villa Comunale**, a green public garden with statues and fountains, which houses the well-known *Stazione Zoologica* (Zoological Institute) and its famous **Acquarius**. The castle stands on a small island formed by the remains of an extinct volcanic cauldron which originally included the Pizzofalcone hill lying behind it. Its history dates back to Roman times when it was built for Lucullus. The first notice of its use as a fortification dates back to the 12th century when mention is made of a stronghold, later enlarged, which was adapted from an ancient monastic hermitage. The castle was witness to a long and sensational history; after its adaption by the Angevins (14th century) it suffered frequent bombardment and was almost completely restructured towards the end of the 17th century. The castle's present appearance comes from the high yellowish barriers which act as a natural background to the Santa Lucia harbour. The interior consists of medieval walls and alternates Gothic features with more ancient remains such as the ruins of a place of worship dedicated to *St. Salvatore*. Also worthy of note are the towers known as the *Torre Maestra* and the *Torre Normandia*.

The diamond-shaped ashlar-work which enriches the façade of the Church of Gesù Nuovo.

GESÙ NUOVO SQUARE

This square opens out close to a line formed by numerous roads which divide the town into two equal parts and which is thus known locally as "Spaccanapoli". The long straight road follows in part the ancient lower decuman of the primitive Greek-Roman settlement. The square is very interesting because of the richness of the decorations of the Guglia dell'Immacolata (Virgin Mary's Spire) and those of the Church of Gesù Nuovo.

The **Virgin Mary's Spire** is in fact one of the most noted Parthenopean sights. The tall slender outline crowned by an effigy of the *Virgin Mary* in gilded bronze dominates the square from the height of its 30 m. Its construction was undertaken by Giuseppe di Fiore in the first part of the 18th century, based on a project drawn up by Giuseppe Genuino. The construction, one of the happiest expressions of Neapolitan Baroque, is enriched by sculptures of noteworthy artistic value carried out by Matteo Bottiglieri and Francesco Pagano.

The **Church of Gesù Nuovo** forms an elegant backdrop to the Virgin Mary's Spire. It is also known as the *Chiesa della Trinità Maggiore* and is the result of a transformation which took place in the years bridging the 16th and 17th centuries on the Renaissance Sanseverino Palace. Conspicuous traces of the original building can be seen in the façade with its decorations in piperno with diamond-shaped ashlar-work. The interior, on a grand scale, is in the form of a Greek cross which shows up the triple partition of the nave. The present dome is the result of modifications which have taken place over the centuries after the original one was destroyed by the 1688 earthquake. Among the more noteworthy pieces of artistic work we would mention a fresco by Solimena *(Heliodorus Driven from the Temple)*, some paintings by Luca Giordano *(Scenes from the Life of St. Francesco Saverio)*, the massive presbytery with its vault covered in frescoes by Massimo Stanzione, and a precious wooden shrine which has gilded sculptures by Domenico di Nardo.

The Church of Gesù Nuovo: detail of the tympanum above the portal and a view of the huge interior.

CHURCH AND CLOISTER OF ST. CLARE

The present appearance of the church is due to accurate restoration work carried out to repair the damage caused to it by heavy bombing on August 4th, 1943. It has thus been restored to its Provençal-Gothic origins after the fire provoked by the bombardment had largely cancelled the signs of subsequent additions and Baroque transformations carried out in the 18th century by Domenico Antonio Vaccaro. The first church was completed in 1310 on the wishes of Robert of Anjou and his wife Sancia of Majorca. The large single-naved interior is illuminated by slender single-lobed windows. Two rows of side chapels are framed by large Gothic arches resting on robust columns. Among the works of art to be found here we would mention the *Tomb of Robert I of Anjou* (14th century) which is the work of the Florentine artists Giovanni and Pacio Bertini; some works by Tino di Camaino (*Tomb of Mary of Valois, Tomb of Charles Duke of Calabria*) and the *Tomb of Agnes and Clementine of Durazzo* by Antonio Baboccio (14th century). The famous **Cloister**

of the Poor Clares is part of the convent building. The large garden is surrounded on its four sides by an arcade with Gothic arches held up by octagonal trachyte pillars. The cross-vaults and walls conserve remnants of 18th-century frescoes which have recently been restored. However the feature of greatest artistic interest is without doubt the beautiful decorations formed by the valuable 18th-century majolica tiles which cover the columns supporting the pergola in the central portion and the backs of the numerous seats. The subjects of these decorations were inspired by the artistic genius of Domenico Antonio Vaccaro and carried out by Donato and Giuseppe Massa and depict mythological, rural, landscape, and Carnival motifs and masked figures.

Cloisters of The Poor Clares: some pictures of the lovely majolics.

CATHEDRAL

The Naples Cathedral, known locally as the *Church of St. Januarius*, has Angevin origins (13th-century) although the actual building is the result of numerous transformations and alterations over the centuries. This is particularly evident in its façade with its elegant modern neoGothic additions (19th-20th century), but not the doors which are the work of Antonio Baboccio assisted by Tino di Camaino and the students of Nicola Pisano. Its imposing monumental interior is divided by pilasters surrounded by numerous columns supporting the elegant Gothic arches. The outstanding wooden ceiling has painted panels while the walls of the central nave are covered in frescoes by Luca Giordano. F. Grimaldi's 17th-century *Chapel of St. Januarius* houses the relics of the patron saint; the *Chapel of St. Restituta* was once a 14th-century Basilica; the Renaissance *Carafa* (or *Succorpo*, set under the apse) *Chapel* and the lovely *Baptismal Font* are all worth a visit.

◄ *Church of St. Januarius: view of the neo-Gothic façade.*

Church of St. Januarius: a prospect of the huge interior and a view of the baptismal font.

A prospect of the building which houses the National Archaeological Museum.

NATIONAL ARCHEOLOGICAL MUSEUM

The vast artistic collection, mainly referring to the Greek-Roman civilisation, is laid out in a capacious building which can be easily recognised by its red exterior. Built in the late 16th century the palace was originally constructed as a barracks and was later used as a university. Its transformation to museum came about during the first part of the 19th century. The first nucleus of the museum was founded almost a century earlier by Charles of Bourbon who wished to house the Farnese collection, passed down to him with his mother's inheritance. But the subsequent enlargement of the huge artistic patrimony by the additions from the archaeological excavations at Pompeii, Herculaneum and Stabiae, made it necessary to move to the present building.

Since it would be impossible to list all the exhibits which make the National Archaeological Museum of Naples one of the most authoritative and prestigious in the world, we will limit ourselves to mentioning just a few of the works which are of major artistic value. On the *ground floor* are to be found the marble sculptures, often copied during the Roman era from the original Greek figures. Apart from the famous *Farnese Bull* (2nd-3rd century A.D.) the collection includes the *Doryphoros*, copied from the original by Policlitus (5th century B.C.), the *Tyrannicides* copied from the 5th-century B.C. original, the *Callipige Venus* again copied from the Greek original. In the *mezzanine* the mosaics from Pompeii and paintings are on display. We would like to mention here the following: *The Battle of Isso, Plato's Academy, Portrait of a Lady*, and the famous statuette *Dancing Faun*. On the *first floor* the finds from the *Villa dei Papiri* at Herculaneum are on display. Mention should be made of the *bronze statuettes*, the *paintings* from Herculaneum, Pompeii and Stabiae, the *Farnese Cup* and the sculptures of *Sleeping Satyr* and the *Farnese Atlas*. On the *second floor* (partially undergoing renovation) one may admire the collection of vases, especially the extremely interesting one of Etruscan, Attic, Lucan and Apulan origin and those from the Campana region.

CARTHUSIAN MONASTERY OF ST. MARTIN

This building is situated on the summit of the Vomero hill in a magnificent panoramic position overlooking the city, the gulf and the islands. Its characteristic outline, shadowed by the imposing structure of St. Elmo's Castle, is one of the most notable sights of the Neapolitan scenery. The monastery was begun during the Angevin era and was completed during the reign of Joan I (second part of the 14th century). The first architects to work on the construction were F. di Vito, M. di Malotto, T. di Camaino, A. Primario and B. de Baeza. The building was restructured in the late 16th century by G.A. Dosio but was completely transformed by G.G. Conforto and G. Fanzago who gave it a typically Neapolitan-Baroque style during the 17th century. The **National Museum of St. Martin** offers an interesting cross-section of the city's history and art during the 17th to 19th centuries. The beautiful **Church** with its single nave amazes one by the richness of its marble decorations and can be considered an art gallery in its own right. Finally we would draw your attention to the **Large Cloister** which is the work of G.A. Dosio and C. Fanzago and the **Procurators' Cloister** also by Dosio.

Two views of the Carthusian Monastery of St. Martin.

Some vistas of St. Elmo's Castle.

CASTEL ST. ELMO
(ST. ELMO'S CASTLE)

St. Elmo's Castle is certainly the most panoramic of all the Neapolitan fortresses. Its enormous walls tower over the Vomero hill and seem to protect the underlying *Carthusian Monastery of St. Martin.* The central nucleus which is partially dug out of the hillside is surrounded by a circle of bastions which give it its star-shaped form. Its construction was begun during the Angevin period (first part of the 14th century) and various architects who were occupied in the city at that time became involved, and also contributed to the nearby Monastery. The castle was originally known as *Belforte* and its present title derives from the name Erasmo which has become modified over the centuries. In fact a place of worship dedicated to that saint in the 10th century stood where the castle now stands. At the beginning of the 16th century Pedro of Toledo, viceroy of Spain arranged for it to undergo substantial changes. Together with the other Neapolitan castles St. Elmo's Castle suffered historical vicissitudes and underwent numerous seiges, was fought over by the various dominating powers and withstood frequent popular uprisings, among which the legendary Masaniello revolt (1647).

Today the castle is a military prison but even in the past it had been used as a detention centre. Among its more illustrious prisoners the names of Tommaso Campanella, Mario Pagano, Ettore Carafa, Pietro Colletta, Silvio Spaventa and Carlo Poerio stand out. The 16th-century *Church of St. Elmo* and the *Chapel of St. Mary of Pilar* (17th century) form part of the structure. From the paths and the square above the castle one has an extensive panorama over the city framed by Vesuvius, over the Parthenopean countryside and over the wonderful gulf with views of Capri and the outline of the Flegrean Islands.

From the walls of St. Elmo's Castle there is a wide panorama. The photo below shows the massive Gothic shape of the Church of St. Clara which rises out of the sea of houses in the old part of the town. At the centre of the picture is the long straight road popularly known as "Spaccanapoli".

A lovely picture of the Capodimonte Royal Palace. The ► building houses the Museum and National Gallery of Capodimonte and stands in a beautiful setting in the park of the same name.

THE CAPODIMONTE ROYAL PALACE

The magnificent building is beautifully positioned in an extensive park at the top of the Capodimonte hill. The plans for its construction were drawn up by G. Antonio Medrano), charged with the task by Charles of Bourbon who wished to house the Farnese art collection there. The work was begun in 1738 but nearly a century passed before it was finished. The proportions of the palace are extremely harmonious and are enhanced by the slender parastas in piperno which contrast with the pale red of its external walls.

Inside there are the important **Museum and National Gallery of Capodimonte** which were reorganized in the 1950's. Among the illustrious artists represented here are Simone Martini (*St. Ludovico of Toulouse)*; Masolino da Panicale (*The Assumption*); Masaccio (*The Crucifixion*); Botticelli (*Virgin and Child with Angels*); Sebastiano del Piombo (*Holy Family and St. John*); Correggio (*Gypsy Girl*); Giovanni Bellini (*Transfiguration*); Mantegna (*Portrait of Francesco Gonzaga*); Tiziano (*Portrait of Paolo III Farnese*); Caravaggio (*The Flagellation*); Pieter Brueghel (*Parable of the Blind Men*); Lucas Cranach (*Christ and the Adulteress*); and El Greco (*Youth Blowing on a Burning Coal*).

In the so-called **Eighteenth-Century Gallery** there are some

A panorama of Naples and its gulf framed by Vesuvius: the picture synthesizes the difficult equilibrium between the natural surroundings and the works of man.

A characteristic souvenir stall.

paintings by artists from the last century, mainly Neapolitan artists but also from other Italian schools, together with artists from abroad. The section of the gallery known as the **Historical Wing and Museum**, houses a valuable collection of porcelain from both the city, and abroad. The *De Ciccio collection* of Italian and foreign porcelain and majolica from the 13th to 18th centuries is also well worth a visit as is the so-called *Porcelain Room* which dates from the late 18th century. In the **Park**, also known as the *Capodimonte Wood*, is the 18th-century building which housed the famous *Capodimonte porcelain factory*.

POSILLIPO

The magnificent Posillipo hill is one of Naples' loveliest residential areas and consists of a ridge formed from tufa which is the remains of an ancient crater active during the volcanic manifestations which upset the nearby Flegrean region. The series of parks and beautiful homes, interspersed with coves and inlets, and enriched by beautiful views of the gulf, make this angle of the city between *Marechiaro* and *Mergellina* a corner of paradise which harmonises well with its name of evident Greek extraction (*Pausilypon* = that which eases pain). The Roman **Villa Pausilypon**, originally the property of Vedius Polliones and then belonging to Augustus, stood on this spot and traces have been found of numerous public buildings which were a part of it. Near to the typical Neapolitan seaside village of **Marechiaro**, with its lovely view, is a building which has been made famous by a Neapolitan song. To this day the lapid perpetuating the memory of the famous window immortalised in the song by Salvatore di Giacomo "A Marechiaro" and set to music by F.P. Tosti can be seen.

Posillipo: The famous window at Marechiaro and a picture of the seaside town of the same name, two aspects of picturesque Naples.

Popular paintings frequently show us scenes of the Gulf of Naples framed in the smoking outline of Vesuvius, whether they are modern postcards or antique paintings and etchings, but we must not forget that this active volcano is a reality, and is situated only 12 kms to the southeast of the city. Similarly, since Vesuvius is an integral part of the Neapolitan countryside it has perforce conditioned the history and way of life of a vast territory.

This unique example on the European continent of an active volcano has a truncated-conical outline and a complex morphological structure. The volcanic mechanism of Vesuvius, which is of the enclosed type, has two distinct and well-defined morphological parts: *Mount Somma* and *Vesuvius* itself. The former represents the original volcanic structure and is 1132 m. high, while the second, also known as the *Big Cone*, is situated inside the large enclosure, positioned slightly off-centre towards the south and presently arrives at a height of 1172 m. The rim of Mount Somma's crater has a circumference of almost 11 kms, while that of Vesuvius measures about 1500 m. The Big Cone is separated from Mount Somma's volcanic enclosure by the so-called *Giant's Valley* which in turn is divided into the *Horse's Yard* (to the west) and the *Valley of Hell* (to the east).

The volcano which was formed geologically in the late Pleistocene age boasts a long activity which can be resumed in four phases: The *primitive, ancient* and *recent* stages of the *Somma* and *Vesuvius*. Among its more notable eruptions, of which we have definite testimony, is that of August 24th in the year 79 A.D. which razed Pompeii, Herculaneum and Stabiae to the ground, and those of the years 472, 685, 1036, 1139, 1631, 1737, 1794, 1822, 1855, 1858, 1861, 1872, 1906, 1929. The last eruption, that of March 1944, destroyed the villages of St. Sebastiano al Vesuvio and Massa di Somma, exposing in no uncertain terms the dangers of the excessive urbanisation which was taking place on the slopes of the volcano. This still continues today in an unexpected measure, as if to renew man's eternal challenge with the restless mountain.

A view of Vesuvius.

A picturesque view of Capri as seen from the ▶ peninsular of Sorrento.

THE ISLAND OF CAPRI

The island which is frequently linked to the mainland (Naples and Sorrento) by boats and hovercraft is only 5 kms from Punta Campanella, which represents the furthermost point of the Sorrento peninsular. Its population (12.500 approx.) is spread out over the two Comunes of Capri and Anacapri. The total surface area is around 11 square kms and measures approximately 6 kms in length and at its widest point measures around 3 kms. The circumference of its coasts measures 17 kms.

The island is set in front of the Sorrento peninsular, from which it is separated by a narrow strait of water called Bocca Piccola. The geological structure of Capri is prevalently calcarea with the presence of tufa and pozzuolana transported by the winds during the paroxysmal vulcanic eruptions of the Flegrean Fields and Vesuvius. The coasts which are high and rocky offer a large number of grottoes and are surrounded by rocks which rise out of the water, such as the famous Faraglioni. The highest mountains are Mount Solaro (589 m) Mount St. Maria (499 m) and Mount Tiberius (335 m). Of the many versions given for the origin of the place-name - *Caprea* according to Strabone, to indicate the harsh conformation of its rocky soil, or *Capraim* which comes from a semitic expression which means "two villages" - *Capreae* is without doubt the more convincing because it would refer as Varrone ascertaines, to the considerable presence of wild boars on the island (*Caprios* according to Greek spelling). The fact that Capri was a Greek colony is now certain even if it is believed that it was populated as far back as the Paleolithic age. The Roman "discovery" of Capri dates back to 29 B.C. when Augustus landed here on his way back to Rome after the Eastern campaigns. After the death of Augustus (14 A.D.) his successor Tiberius, made Capri his "golden exile', choosing the island as his home for the last decade of his life. His death (37 A.D.) which took place near the Villa of Lucullus at Miseno, whilst he was trying to reach his beloved island, marked the beginning of the decline of Capri. At the fall of the Roman Empire Capri was controlled by the abbots of Montecassino and by Neapolitans, and was subjected to frequent pirate raids especially those of the Saracens. Then it was controlled by the Longobards who were followed by the Normans and then the island passed from one domination to another including the Aragonese, Angevins, and the raids of the Turkish pirates Kahir ad-Din (*Barbarossa*) and Dragut. For a long time it came under Spanish administration and suffered a great plague (18th century), and then finally it was governed by the Bourbons. It was contended by the French and English at the time of the Napoleonic Wars, after which it was ruled once more by the Bourbons of Naples before its annexation to the newly formed Kingdom of Italy thereby estabilishing the characteristics which it now maintains as one of the obligatory stages of international tourism.

MARINA GRANDE

Here, in the Augustian age there was a sandy shore, the *Grande Marina* which the Romans used as a landing place for their ships and which afterwards became a port, situated in a more easternly location than the present infrastructure in harmony with *Punta Vivara*, from where one reached the imperial residence of **Palazzo a Mare** (Palace on the Sea). The traces of this ancient maritime landing place, fortified and reinforced by Tiberius who wanted to facilitate communications between it and the fleet which was quartered in the roadstead of Miseno can still be seen today and give testimony of the important role of the island in the most splendid era of the Roman Empire, between the first century B.C. and the first century A.D. Today Marina Grande is a beautiful riverside town which is set in a lovely natural position at the foot of the green saddle along which the romantic town of Capri stretches. The town of Marina Grande has merged with the above lying main town; in the small square which overlooks the port and which is usually swarming with tourists stand the characteristic houses of Capri, rendered typical by the terraces, the balconies, the open galleries and the multi-coloured façades of the town, brightened by the "Pompeian red" which is one of the most intense notes of colour along the whole Neapolitan coast.

The first sensations felt by the tourist, the first contact with this unique island, are of a fairytale nature: one's gaze, which is at first drawn to the picturesque port, the boats and the sequence of enchanting houses, is then directed to the green slopes which dominate Marina and which allow one to catch a glimpse of the first few houses on Capri, on the summit of the saddle. Amidst the steep terraced slopes, covered with an exuberant and blooming Mediterranean flora, or otherwise covered with vines, stands out the marvellous foliage of the maritime pines, whilst the white houses scenically set out in the shape of an amphitheatre on the background of the steep crags of calcareous rocks all contribute to form a part of this wonderful Mediterranean crib.

Each end of the port of Marina Grande has imposing wharfs; at the end of the western wharf there is a *Column* with a Corinthian capital, placed on a high pedestal and this is proof of the important significance (even felt today) of the Roman presence on Capri. In the eastern part of the port a modern, well-equipped tourist dock is used by the sailors and by the beautiful boats which help to underline the tourist "enigma" and worldwide fame of this dream island.

However the most "vivid" aspect of Marina Grande is the large number of fishing boats, moored along the waters of the shore line or beached along the shore. Here, in front of the houses (which were once used as ware-houses) the fishermen of the island carry out their work, either mending their multicoloured boats or repairing their nets while they wait for the most favourable moment to set sail.

The boat trip around the island, like the visits to the numerous **Grottes** and to the **Faraglioni** can only be carried out when weather conditions, the sea and the tides permit.

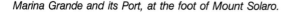

Marina Grande and its Port, at the foot of Mount Solaro.

The panoramic look-out post.

On the following pages: Capri's famous small Square ("Piazzetta"), a noted tourist place on the island.

CAPRI

This is the main town and the major centre of the island and stretches along the saddleback which lies between Mount St. Maria, Mount Tuoro and Mout Tiberius. The *Umberto I Square* is universally known as the "**Piazzetta**": it is the throbbing heart of the main town as well as being the main tourist attraction of the island. Once known as the "little theatre of the world" it is really the "drawing room" of Capri; at the tables of the cafès, which are shaded by multicoloured and characteristic sunshades, the most important and prestigious people from the world of the cinema, fashion, literature, and politics and the composite world of business have sat.

It is an important meeting point and an obligatory stop for the crowds of tourists who come here throughout the whole year. The small square opens out on the site where the first Greek colonies established the acropolis, between the 5th and the 4th centuries B.C. Imposing traces of the ancient tombs of Capri, built in the Greek period are still visible near the mountain cablecar station, inserted amongst the houses and the town perimetry which has a Medieval plan. The small square is dominated by the

Clocktower, once the belltower of the ancient cathedral, and has a small cupola which has a decidedly eastern stamp, under which small arcades which house the bells open out. At one end of this charming centre lies the **Town Hall**, once the residence of the Bishops, which has a façade covered with plaques, whilst opposite this building stands the animated façade of the **Church of St. Stephen** which can be reached by a small flight of steps. Beyond the Clocktower, the square opens out onto the small *Belvedere* loggia, characterized by a succession of white columns placed on high pedestals. From the parapet of the small loggia one can admire one of the most spectacular views of the whole island, which stretches out from the unmistakable profile of Ischia to the Flegrean region and the whole Neapolitan gulf, dominated by the menacing outline of Vesuvius. The views is particularly enchanting in the late evening when the numerous lights of Capri are seen against the dark profile of the mountains, softened by the twilight, making an enchanting fairylike picture which is almost like a Christmas crib.

THE CHURCH OF ST. STEPHEN

The building which we see today is the result of a late 17th century project presided over by the architect Picchiatti and brought to completion by Marziale Desiderio of Amalfi. The exterior of the building (which stands on the site of a primitive cathedral, of which only the *Clocktower* remains) is characterized by its façade, enlivened by the curvilinear architecture upon which are inserted some tambours, these being surmounted by beautiful eastern-style cupolas. The building is dominated by a central dome, opened at the base by a series of arched windows. The façade, consisting of two orders, has a decidedly Baroque aspect, as can be seen by the curvilinear trend of the upper order, enriched by ornamental motifs. The upper order, vertically scanned by pilaster strips has two large niches containing statues. The most important artistic element that one can admire inside the church is the floor under the main altar: this is of a series of colourful pieces brought here from the *Villa Jovis*, the most celebrated of the many villas of Tiberius. In the Chapel of the Rosary pieces of another Roman floor have been set out, which, in all probability were transferred from another Roman residence: the *Villa of Tragara*. Amongst the other works of artistic interest, the funeral monuments of the Arcucci should be noted. These were carried out by the Florentine sculptor Michelangelo Naccherino (16th - 17th century), and also a picture dating back to the 16th century depicting the *Madonna and Child with Saints Michael and Anthony*.

CERIO PALACE

The building is situated at the extreme end of a square which bears the same name, near the Church of St. Stephen. The building which is reached by a flight of steps is characterized by an arcade on the ground floor; here there once stood a fortress which dated back to the Angevin period (14th century) and which later underwent radical changes and restructuring. Inside the building the *Ethnological Centre of Capri* can be found. A great amount of the material on show here was discovered by the doctor and naturalist Ignazio Cerio who was amongst the first to undertake excavation work at the beginning of this century.

THE MEDIEVAL DISTRICT

All around the famous Small Square and beyond the Church of St. Stephen, a complex maze of lanes and narrow alleys testify the presence of a Medieval borough on Capri.
Once again the dominant colour is the whiteness of the house fronts, which are for the greater part built of calcareous stone and tufaceous material.
Amongst the most important architectural buildings of the Medieval district we find the 17th century **Church of Salvatore**, built by Dionisio Lazzari, which, with the adjoining *Convent of the Tertiary*, forms a structural unity which is typical of the 17th century. The picturesque little **Church of St. Anna** (12th century) looks out onto a small courtyard and in fact makes up a structural unity with the adjoining houses.

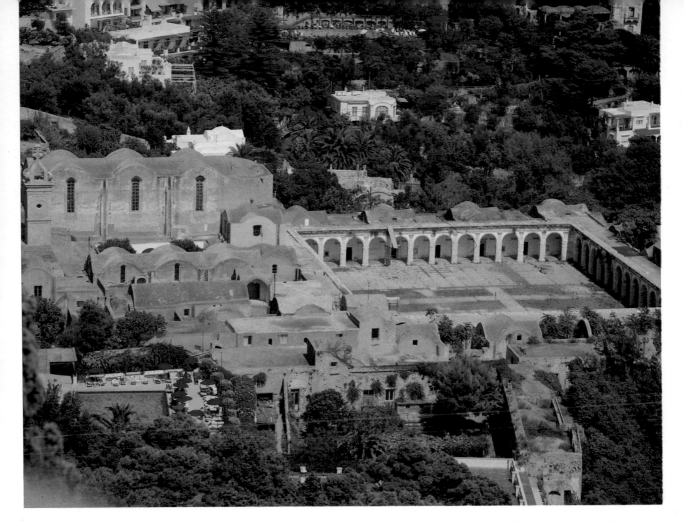

◄ *A breathtaking aerial view of via Krupp.*

The Charterhouse of St. James.

VIA KRUPP

The panoramic road, which can only be undertaken on foot because of its narrow dimensions is one of the most noted attractions of this pleasant Mediterranean "gem". It was built at the beginning of this century by the famous German industrialist whose name has been given to the road itself. Picturesquely cut into the rocks which characterize the rocky cliffs of the southern coast of Capri, it goes from the *Gardens of Augustus* to *Marina Piccola*. Further down a Saracean **Tower** commemorates the ancient fights for the possession of the island.

THE CHARTERHOUSE OF ST. JAMES

The founding of the Charterhouse was sponsored, in the second half of the 14th century by Giacomo Arcucci, secretary to Joan I, Queen of Naples and the Count of Alta-mura and Minervino. The most ancient parts of the monastic complex can be found around the *Little Cloisters*, graced by elegant arches which stand on small columns, by cross vaults and brightened up by the oleanders, which surround the central well-curb, dominated by the Baroque cusp of the so-called *Clocktower*. This part of the charterhouse, where we can find the *Church* and the *Refectory* imitates the trend of the Cistercian monastic architecture whilst the *Great Cloister*, the product of a 16th-century addition, denotes structural affinities with that of the Neapolitan charterhouse of San Martino.

The Church, which has only one nave, maintains an extremely bare and linear aspect. Worthy of note is the beautiful doorway, which is Gothic (ogival) in style, in whose lunette is a frescoe of the 14th century depicting *The Virgin and Child with Saint Brunone and Saint James with Queen Joan and Count Arcucci*. In the buildings near the Church can be seen the **Museum of the Charterhouse** which contains, amongst other things, sculptures which have been severely corroded by the salt water of the Blue Grotto.

45

FARAGLIONI

Emerging from the unfathomable depths of an extraordinary and intensely blue sea, these enigmatic colossi of rocks have always constituted the most famous and popular image of Capri throughout the world. Even though, in other places, other rocks of a similar form and dimension are called by the same name, those of Capri, are the

Faraglioni "par excellence".

Situated in front of the south-eastern coast of the island they were formed by the age-old erosion of the waters which broke off "walls" of rock from the central body of the island and also formed cracks, cavities, grotoes and beautiful natural arches, moreover the relentless action of the erosion which took place can be seen all along the coast of Capri, especially in this region.

Subdivided into *Faraglioni of the Earth*, the *Middle Faraglioni* and the *Outer Faraglioni* they reach a height of respectively 111, 81 and 105 m. Nearby, in front of the so-called Porto di Tragara, stands the "Scoglio del Monacone". A favourite spot with photographers, they are easily reached by boat and make up one of the obligatory stops on the journey around the island. Their waters, limpid and profound, are a paradise for all those interested in nature and underwater diving; on the outer Faraglione lives the rare *Lacerta coerula faraglionensis*.

The imposing majesty of the Faraglioni of Capri never cease to amaze the visitor.

Two enchanting views of the Natural Arch and the Grotto of Matermania.

THE NATURAL ARCH

This strange natural phenomenon, together with the Faraglioni and the Grotto of Matermania is one of the most famous tourist spots on this part of the island. One gains access to the Arch by a flight of steps which branches off a path frequented by tourists. This itinerary describes a sort of circular trip around Mount Tuoro leading out from the centre of Capri to the houses on the outskirts of Matermania, along via Camarelle, via Tragara and via Matermania.

GROTTO OF MATERMANIA

Following the scenic itinerary which broadens out in front of the natural beauty of the Faraglioni, one goes upwards to the Cove of the Fig Tree, at a height where, stretched out along the narrow Punta di Massullo, the unmistakable profile of the *Red House* stands out. This villa was once owned by the Tuscan writer Curzio Malaparte.
A little further ahead a fork in the road leads to the Grotto of Matromania. Also known as the *Grotto of Matermania* it is a natural cavity where the ancient orgiastic customs

Marina Piccola, with the bathing resorts and the Rock of the Sirens.

were practised. These rites were part of the worshipping of the *Mater Magna* , and were also frequently carried out on the Sorrento peninsula at the height of the Imperial Age and were similar to those of Cybele. In its present state the grotto shows the elaborative work which was carried out by the Romans, who reinforced the natural vaults with walls and decorated the grotto with mosaics and stucco work of which only scarse and fragmentary traces remain.

MARINA PICCOLA

Marina Piccola has its own particular character, more cosy, graceful and attractive; alongside its delightful coves, between the 1950 - 1960's, the reputation of Capri as a tourist Mecca flourished. This "boom" was thanks to the presence on the island of the most famous names of the film world, the cultural world and that of show business. However there are numerous indications that the place was populated as far back as the most remote ages. Along the rocky spurs which are outlined along the eastern side of Mount Solaro, one finds the *Grotto of the Ferns* which dominates the underlying Marina and which represents one of the most important prehistoric sites of the whole island. Archeological excavations have brought

to light a numerous quantity of domestic objects as well as the remains of funeral objects and primitive ceramic objects. This grotto, populated as far back as the Neolithic Bronze Age, acted as an important lookout post along the southern coast. In the Imperial Age, the Romans used it to reinforce the characteristics of the natural landing place; some building work done on the ancient Roman port are still visible today near the so-called *Rock of the Sirens*.

Today the enchanting vision of Marina Piccola can be enjoyed by those who reach it by means of either the road which bears the same name, or by the evocative Via Krupp. The delightful "Rock of the Sirens" (or "of the Mule") forms a natural barrier between the *Marina di Mulo* which stretches out in a westerly direction up to the Point bearing the same name, and the *Marina di Pennauto* which stretches to the east up to the powerful outline of the Faraglione. In addition to the numerous tourist and seaside infrastructures Marina Piccola has typical restaurants and fashionable "haunts" such as the famous "Canzone del Mare" ("Song of the Sea") which during the "roaring" years of the Cinema became one of the meeting points for artists of world renown.

Marina Piccola is one of the main starting points from where one sets out along the journey around the island.

◄ *At Capri many wide caves open out in the rocks.*

A view of Castiglione Castle.

CASTIGLIONE CASTLE

The climb up to the panoramic spot of Castiglione is without doubt amongst the most worthwhile if only for the enjoyment of the spectacular scenic view which can be seen in the direction of the Faraglioni and towards the towns of Capri, which emerge from the Mediterranean scrub, wonderfully set round in the shape of an amphitheatre along the slopes of the natural saddle which separates Marina Grande from Marina Piccola.

This pleasant excursion allows one to observe in all their entirety, the unadulterated buildings of marked Medieval influence which make up one of the most characteristic and important examples of the ancient urban arrangements of the historical centre of Capri. Castiglione Castle, as one sees it today has the characteristics bestowed on it by restoration work which was only finished in quite recent times. The powerful embattled ramparts and the huge square reinforcement towers, which are also surmounted by a crown of merlons, stand on the summit of a rocky peak. The side of the building which faces the sea seems to fall in steep crags and cliffs of bare rock in which the gigantic Grotto of Castiglione can be seen, down towards the sea, whilst the side facing the Charterhouse of St.

James is covered by a thick verdant undergrowth, from which some magnificent and typical residences seem to peep out at one.

Castiglione Castle was originally a Medieval structure, built on the site of an ancient Greek acropolis. During the numerous pirate raids the Castle was an important defensive rampart for the population of Capri (even though most of the population used to take shelter in the *Grotto of Castiglione*. This grotto, which had been a prehistoric seat since the Neolithic era, was used by the Romans as a temple, connected to an *Imperial Villa* above the grotto. At the Villa one can make out the remains of walls in *opus reticulatum*.

This magnificent villa, which stands on the northern slopes of Castiglione, was discovered at the end of the 18th century by the Austrian archeologist Norbert Hadrawa. It seems that in numerous rooms, later hidden by a disasterous attempt to cover up the villa, a large amount of interesting and valuable exhibits were found, such as mosaic and marble floors, frescoes and stucco decorations which were unfortunately lost after the plundering of the Villa by Hadrawa himself.

A view of the southern coast towards Marina Piccola.

The main entrance to Villa Jovis.

VILLA JOVIS

The majestic remains of a magnificent Roman villa dating back to the Imperial Age stand above the plateau which culminates in the so-called Mount Tiberius (335 m). The Villa which bears the name of the most important of the Olympian divinities is the most representative of a consistent number of villas built on Capri during the Augustan-Tiberian eras.

A written tradition, quoted by Tacitus would attribute Augustus' successor with the building of twelve imperial residences all dedicated to the Consenting Gods (Jupiter, Apollo, Neptune, Mars, Vulcan, Mercury, Juno, Minerva, Venus, Vesta, Ceres and Diana).

From the centre of Capri, taking first the via Sopramonte and then the via Tiberius which leads into the via Moneta one can easily reach the spot where the Villa stands.

A little before the ruins of the Villa Jovis, on the right, stand the broken remains of another Roman tower. Here, there once stood a *Lighthouse Tower*, an ancient light system used for signalling by either fire or smoke. During Tiberius' stay on Capri, this structure was particularly important as it permitted the Emperor to have daily com-

munication with the mainland, by means of a beam situated on the facing Punta Campanella, at the extremity of the Sorrento peninsular. In such a way Tiberius decided the destiny of the Empire during the last years of his tormented reign.

From the same tower contact was also kept with the lighthouse of Capo Miseno, in whose roadstead the imperial fleet rode at anchor. Due to a strange coincidence the Lighthouse Tower crumbled during sismic tremors a little while before the death of Tiberius; it was later restored and used as a lighthouse to defend the ships of the island up until the 17th century.

There have been many discussions about the figure of Tiberius, discussions which more often than not linger over details of his supposed vices and perversions rather than on his virtues and qualities as a ruler of the boundless Empire of Rome. We should not forget however, that many of the anecdotes, which refer to the successor of Augustus, whether they are true or not, are, the result of stories told by narrators who were clearly biased and definitely hostile towards Tiberius. It would therefore be ap-

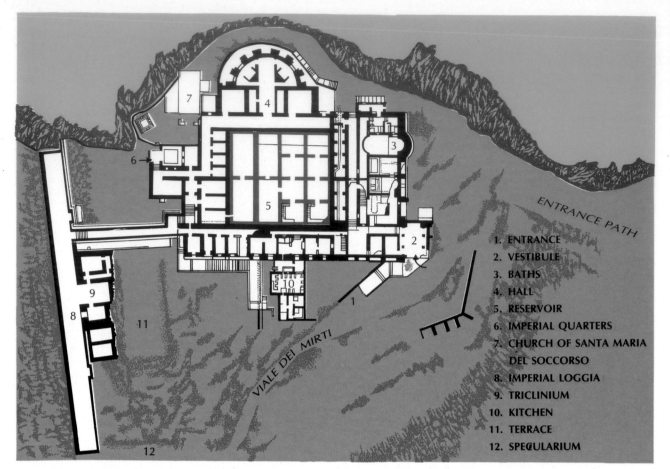

1. ENTRANCE
2. VESTIBULE
3. BATHS
4. HALL
5. RESERVOIR
6. IMPERIAL QUARTERS
7. CHURCH OF SANTA MARIA
   DEL SOCCORSO
8. IMPERIAL LOGGIA
9. TRICLINIUM
10. KITCHEN
11. TERRACE
12. SPECULARIUM

propriate to reflect, separating fiction from fact, on the terrible punishments which he inflicted on families and servants whom he felt were unloyal, on the capital punishments carried out by throwing his enemies into a bottomless abyss (known today as *Tiberius' Leap*) as well as the slaughtering of young men and women which took place in the Blue Grotto after the licentious erotic games in which both sexes took part. Concerning these facts Axel Munthe writes (*The History of St. Michael* Publishers: Garzanti, 1940) "... As to the sinister traditions of Tiberius, handed down through the ages by the *Annals* of Tacitus the ,detractor of humanity' as Napoleon called him, I said to Lord Dufferin that History had never made such a big mistake as when it condemned this great Emperor to such infamy only on the testimony of his greatest accusers. Tacito is a splendid writer but his *Annals* are historical fiction, not History... That Tacitus himself didn't believe the stories about the orgies on Capri is clear from his own narrative, since he doesn't play down to even one degree his general conception of Tiberius as a great Emperor and as a great man ,of admirable character and much respected' to use his own words. Even his much less intelligent follower, Suetonius recounts the most filthy stories, making the observations that it is hardly admissable that they should be told let alone believed... Tiberius was 68 when he retired to Capri with a reputation for having led a strict and moral life still intact, and not even damaged by his worst enemies. The possible diagnosis of senile dementia can be excluded, because all the

historians maintain that the old man was in full possession of his faculties and was physically fit until his death at the age of 79. Moreover the streak of madness which ran through Julian's family was absent in that of Claudius. His life on the island was that of a solitary old man, a tired ruler of an ungrateful world, a gloomy idealist with a shattered and bitter heart (today one could call him a hypochondriac), but a man with a magnificent intellect and rare spirit who still had faith in humanity. It is little wonder that he had no trust in his contemporaries and that he hated them because almost all the men and women in whom he had put his trust had betrayed him...".

The principle nucleus of Villa Jovis or *Palazzo di Tiberio* (Tiberius' Palace) stands on the summit of the most extreme eastern slope of Capri, in a scenario of inexpressible beauty. Above the ruins rises the small *Church of St. Maria del Soccorso* built on the site of a medieval place of worship dedicated to *St. Christopher* and *St. Leonard*. Nearby is a statue of *The Virgin and Child*, from where one can look out over the whole island, taking in the endless horizon which sweeps from the distant Ischia to the Neapolitan gulf dominated by the characteristic profile of Vesuvius, as far as the nearby Punta Campanella and the wide gulf of Salerno.

The main part of the ancient imperial construction revolves around the magnifent complex of the *water tanks* which were used to provide water for the entire complex of the Villa collecting the rain water in spacious impluvia. All around are to be found the various interiors which have been discovered and which have a total surface area of over 7000 square metres; it is believed however that the Villa Jovis with its various outlying buildings covered an even vaster area. Particularly interesting are the remains of the wall which sometimes show elements of *opus reticulatum* and sometimes elements of *opus incertum*, whilst often the floors have a herring-pone pattern (*opus spicatum*). At the side of the water tanks the actual *imperial residence* is situated, which leads to the so-called *imperial loggia*. The latter which has a triclinium and exedrae was the spot favoured by Tiberius for his walks.

Another conspicuous portion of the villa is the *baths* which show the classical division of the Roman thermal constructions: *Apodyterium* (changing room), *Frigidarium, Tepidarium*, and *Calidarium*. A complex heating system (hypocaust) was used to heat the waters. Next to the church of St. Maria di Soccorso, right at the edge of the rocky slopes which fall sheer to the sea are the remains of what has mistakenly been called a *Nymphaeum* (where nymphs were worshipped). In reality this was a hemicircular room used as a meeting place where the imperial chancellery held audience.

The ruins of the hemicircular room and the Lighthouse Tower.

Tiberius' Leap: now that the cruelty of the Roman emperor has been forgotten, only the natural beauty of the rocks which drop down into an incredibly clear sea, remain.

THE BATHS OF TIBERIUS

The traces of the Baths of Tiberius consist of a sloping wall which leans against a slope rich in vegetation but liable to slide down, of a small area destined to be used as a dwelling place, of a temple with adjoining exedra, used for fish production and some service structures for a small landing suitably defended by walls against the disintegrating action of the breakers.

Many modifications and transformations carried out over the centuries and the complete absence of a large central nucleus do not allow one to immediately perceive the exact location of the original *Palatium* (palace) of Augustus. We know for certain that the Emperor had a soft spot for the place which is today occupied by the *Houses of the Palace on the Sea* and that the villa which stood here was certainly more sober and less imposing than the sumptuous proportions of the villa that his successor, Tiberius, raised on the brink of the steep precipies which face the Sorrento peninsular.

The *Villa of the Palace on the Sea* is the only one of the numerous imperial villas which is situated close to the sea and which occupies a marittime position as opposed to the traditional elevated positions favoured by the Roman architects who worked on Capri.

Today the Tiberian foundations which are known as the Baths of Tiberius are the only parts which have withstood the onslaught of time and the thoughtless plundering by the Austrian Hadrawa in the 18th century, stripping the Villa of the Palace on the Sea of many architectonic furnishings and artistic decorations.

A panoramic view of the Baths of Tiberius as seen from the small Loggia of the Villa St. Michael; one can clearly make out the transparency of the waters.

THE BLUE GROTTO

The Blue Grotto is counted as being one of the major tourist attractions of Capri. This Karst cavity, together with the equally famous Faraglioni has contributed in spreading the fame of this island all over the world. The most traditional and evocative way of carrying out this excursion, which shouldn't be missed during the course of a visit to Capri, is to take one of the tourist boats or motorboats from the Marina Grande. The visit to the Blue Grotto, which can only be undertaken if weather and sea conditions permit, should take place, if at all possible, in the morning so that one can enjoy the play of light which reflects the marvellous chromatic effects of indescribable fascination and evocativeness.

The Blue Grotto which was a well-known and favourite place with the Romans, fell into oblivion and it became shrouded in fear, mystery and superstition blown out of all proportion by the inhabitants of the island who were convinced that the grotto was a meeting place for witches and that horrifying monsters lived there. It seems quite probable however that an increase of the bradyseismic phenomenon almost closed off the access to the grotto. It was already the subject of much discussion with both scholars and map-readers as far back as the 17th century and was then rediscovered in 1826 by the two daring and bold German travellers, the writer A. Kopisch and the painter E. Fries.

Outside the grotto, whilst waiting patiently to pass through the narrow entrance way, it is possible to observe the remains of the *Villa of Gràdola*. This building, also known as the *Villa of Gradelle* is a Roman construction of secondary importance if one compares it with other, more conspicuous traces of the Imperial era. For a while it lent its name to the grotto which lies below it, before this became known by the name which extols its predominant colours. However the particular predominance that the more well-known imperial residence of the *Villa of Damecuta* assumed in this would support the hypothesis that the Blue Grotto was used by the Romans as a marine temple (where nymphs were worshipped). Such a hypothesis is strenthened by the presence of building work of the Roman period found inside the grotto and by the discovery of sculptures submerged by the bradyseismic actions and corroded by the sea water. Today these statues can be seen inside the Charterhouse Museum of St. James.

The atmosphere of magic seduction inside the Blue Grotto is obtained by the sky-blue reflections of the beams of light which penetrate through the narrow access hole, whilst the extraordinary cobalt-blue transparencies are caused by the light diffused under the mirror of the waters and which filters through an underwater opening. This opening was probably a primeval cavity submerged during ancient tectonic upheavals.

◀ *A view of the interior of the Grotto, which has become famous all over the world.*

A panoramic view towards Anacapri.

ANACAPRI

Splendidly set out along the gentle slopes which descend the steep sides of Mount Solaro, the second most important centre on Capri is set out like on oil stain on the vast thickly-cultivated plateau, in a context of shimmering Mediteranean beauty. It was an elevated settlement during the Greek presence on the island and was a favourite haunt of the patriarchal Roman families who built numerous villas here; loved and frequented by Tiberius who spent many long periods at the imperial villa of Damecuta, it was also chosen by the illustrious Swedish humanist and medic Axel Munthe as a home. Munthe, in his *The History of St. Michael* has wonderfully captivated and handed down to the following generations, the image of this oneeric and fairytale-like enchantend island. Even today, in spite of transformations undergone due to the huge numbers of tourists, Anacapri has managed to retain its characteristics as a typically elevated centre on a Mediterranean island. The white houses, with their decidedly "Caprese" architectural lines, are set out in their bright splendour (given to them by the whitewashed fronts, by the airy and luminous terraces, by the often curvilinear volutes of the roofs of the buildings). All around, a lush vegetation betrayed by the gardens, by the orchards and by the bowers can be seen, whilst the neighbouring districts are marked by the presence of myrtle, juniper, lentisk, broom and by various other species, alternating with the maritime pine and the Aleppo pine.

Anacapri is an ideal holiday village and a renowned health resort which enjoys the benefits of an extraordinary mild and healthy climate. As a starting point for interesting naturalistic excursions and also history trips, it is clustered around the beautiful **Parish Church of St. Sophia**. This was built during Medieval times and is brightened up by the central cupola, by the small minor cupolas and by the majestic *Clocktower*. The elegant Baroque façade (18th century) in two orders is vertically divided by pilaster strips.

59

VILLA ST. MICHAEL

The architectonically ecletic and extremely heterogeneous construction is situated in the town of Capodimonte, on the edge of a steep slope which falls sheer to the underlying Baths of Tiberius. Included within a fantastic landscape context which offers aspects of touching pleasantness, it stands out thanks to the brightness of its composite architectonic attitude amongst the arrogant greenness of the lush Mediterranean vegetation and the cobalt-blue patches of the marine waters below. On the site where Axel Munthe started to build the villa from 1896 stood a rural dwelling which still today, even if it has been transformed, makes up the central nucleus of the buildings. During excavation work, a great number of the remains of the buildings dating back to the Imperial times were discovered; even today the conspicuous remains of the walls in *opus reticulatum* would support the theory that this site was the ancient seat of the *Villa of Capodimonte*, one of the 12 imperial residences of Augustan-Tiberian foundation.

Today, the Villa which has been left to the Swedish state, is presided over by the well-merited *Foundation of St. Michael* which takes care of the indisputable maintenance work. In the summer season, Swedish scholars and humanists stay here, whilst a series of artistic, literary and cultural workshops are held after the expressed wishes of Axel Munthe: a complete integration of the cultural links between Sweden and Italy.

The *entrance hall* into which one passes through a beautiful doorway surmounted by a semicircular mosaic frieze with a golden background and decorated with marble ornaments, has a mosaic floor depicting the Pompeii motif of *Cave canem*, a sculpted fragment of a Roman sarcophagus and a tombstone with epigraphs.

The *dining-room* is also decorated with an ornamental floor which has a copy of a mosaic of Pompeii and allegorical symbols with Bolognese furnishings in the Renaissance style; also to be seen are the collection of Swedish pewter objects dating from the 18th century.

The *entrance hall* forms part of an inner enclosed garden which brings to mind the ancient Roman residences. Also worthy of mention is the extremely valuable Roman well-crib which dates back to the Republican period and which has many delightful external basreliefs. Some bronze heads/busts are copies of original Greek-Roman works, whilst the walls are decorated with ancient fragments of clay and marble and a series of funeral epigraphs.

The *bedroom* which can be reached by the stairs and the loggia, has a strange iron bedstead in 15th century Sicilian style, furniture belonging to the Florentine Rinascimento, bronze sculptures and a marble basrelief dating from the Imperial period depicting *Apollo playing the lyre*.

In the *French drawing room*, the original edition of the *History of St. Michael* is on view together with numerous translations whereas on one wall the motto of Axel Munthe is painted ("To Dare, to Wish, to Know and to Keep Silent").

The *study*, enhanced by a beautiful mosaic floor of marble, which was probably brought from Rome, holds many valuable and antique objects such as the *Head of a Youth* executed in terracotta, noteable Greek works (dating from the 4th century B.C.) and a *Head of Medusa* which Munthe himself found in the marine depths of the Baths of Tiberius.

The adjacent *Venetian Drawing Room*, characterized by the Rococo Venetian furnishings is separated from the study by a beautiful marble column, sustained by an elaborate capital.

The so-called *Loggia delle Sculture* (Loggia of the Sculptures), opens out onto the delightful view of the bowers: the most important work of art is a marble bust depicting *Tiberius* or his descendant *Germanicus*. Amongst the other statues which are worth mentioning are a Roman reproduction of an original Greek statue dating back to the 4th century, B.C. of *Ulysses*. In the middle of the loggia one finds an exquisite mosaic table, sustained by graceful spiral columns, also decorated by mosaic interlacings. This work is attribuited to the Cosmati, Roman marble workers, who carried out marble work as far back as the 12th century. The *small bower* which culminates in a scenic absidal lookout post from where one can admire an enchanting view over the Neapolitan gulf, over the peninsular of Sorrento and over most of the island. In the surrounding districts obvious traces the imperial Roman villa are evident.

The white *Chapel* dedicated to the archangel of the same name gives the title to the entire complex of St. Michael. It is situated on the ruins of a building dating back to the 10th century. On the side of the entrance hall is a funeral sculpture dating back to the Roman period and depicts the *Virgin and Child*. The interior houses a Rinascimental sculpture in wood representing *St. Michael* and a baptismal font from the 14th century. Nearby the chapel, on a wall facing an extremely pleasant view is placed an Egyptian *Sphinx* in red granite, which dates back to the 11th century B.C. Along the evocative *Avenue of the Cypress Trees*, along which Munthe himself planted frutices taken from the garden of the Villa d'Este near Rome one can observe the basreliefs of the tomb of Lucius Careius (first century B.C.), finally arriving at the atrium to the *kitchen*, where valuable ceramic vases from Faenza, dating back to the 18th century and used for pharmaceutical purposes can be seen.

◄ *The entrance to Villa St. Michael.*

The Loggia delle Sculture (The Loggia of the Sculptures): in the foreground, a copy of Hermes (the original is at Naples).

Ruins in "opus reticulatum" of the Villa of Damecuta.

*Ancient ruins and traces of the Roman presence on the ►
island, in the enchanting background the Faraglioni as
seen from Mount Solaro.*

VILLA OF DAMECUTA

The flat plains of Damecuta stretch out along the north-western portion of the vast plateau of Anacapri. In the Imperial Roman era this area was chosen by the architects of the capital who built a great number of villas and residences. Amogst the many buildings, several of which were in fact farms, those of *Aiano, Montivello, Tiberino* and *Vitareto* stand out. Along the margin of this idyllic scenario on the plateau of Anacapri near the Medieval *Tower of Damecuta* lies the vast archeological area which has rendered traces of one of the most imposing and magnificent Roman villas of the Imperial period: the Villa of Damecuta. The origins of the place name seem to be lost in the times of the Greek colonization of the island; the hypothesis that Damecuta seems to be derived from *Domus Augusti* seems to have no foundation in fact.

The complex vicissitudes of this great imperial building, haunted by the figure of Tiberius and his myth, obscure and worrying but at the same time luminous and fascinating were brought to light at the beginning of the second half of the 1930's. At that time the generosity of Axel Munthe, the owner of the place, allowed the archeologists to procede with the work of salvaging the remains of the ancient building.

It also seems certain that this villa was the first of the Imperial villas of the island to be abandoned; seriously lesioned by the fall of materials of a piroclastic nature from the eruptions of Vesuvius, during the destructive episodes which wiped out Pompeii, Herculaneum and Stabiae (79 A.D.) almost completely submerged by the volcanic material, it fell into decline. Today it offers a place for contemplation for visitors especially the work in *opus reticulatum*, whilst in other places can be found the more simple examples in *opus incertum*. In particular the *Loggia* stands out, facing the steep panoramic brink which falls sheer down to the underlying marine abysses. A little below the embattled **Tower of Damecuta** an imposing fortress in stone blocks, built during the 12th century so as to guard over the moves of the Corsair boats, lies the imperial *Domus*. Here in what must have been the bedroom of the Emperor an acephaleos bust has been found depicting *Narcissus* (nude) a clear example of the refined tastes of Tiberius and his lascivious leanings. It seems certain that the Villa had a flight of steps which led down to the sea, near the modern day Punta di Gràdola and near the entrance to the Blue Grotto, where the remains of another Roman villa are clearly visible.

◄ *A picture of the lovely Sorrento coast.*

Sorrento, a view of the Marina Piccola.

SORRENTO

Set on the peninsula from which it takes its name, Sorrento is worthy of mention in its own right. It is a town of just under 18.000 inhabitants stretching out on a volcanic tufa terrace which plunges down to the coast from high cliffs. The charm and natural beauty of this spot, exalted by the fertile citrus plantations, by the vast panorama over the gulf of Naples, Vesuvius and the Flegrean Fields and Islands, the extraordinarily transparent sea and the intensely clear blue sky, combine to make this town one of the sanctuaries of international tourism. An excellent hotel infrastructure, the remarkable quality of the services offered, and the wide variety of sports, recreation and cultural proposals on hand all go to make this a particularly attractive place to visit.

Although the origins of the name of this town are wrapped in mythology and the legend of the sirens (*Surrentum*), it is a certain fact that the place was chosen by man as far back as the Neolithic age. It was probably colonized by the Greeks, followed by Etruscans, Siracu-

sans and Samnites, before being occupied by the Romans who however were not willingly accepted by its inhabitants, who were constantly on the verge of rebellion. During the Imperial era the Roman patriarchs chose it as one of their favourite holiday places. After suffering Gothic and Byzantine occupations Sorrento managed to escape conquest by the Longobards but had to fight off the Saracenes and invaders from Amalfi. It was taken by the Normans in the first part of the 12th century and tried to overcome them with the help of the Republic of Pisa, but was finally brought into submission by King Roger. Sorely tried by internal contrast and by the struggles with its neighbours, Sorrento had a troubled history, made up of seiges and attempted conquests, up to the time of the founding of the Neapolitan Republic (end of the 18th century). The town was the birthplace of the famous 16th-century poet Torquato Tasso and became well-known as a residential area in the 18th century.

PIAZZA TASSO (TASSO SQUARE)

Piazza Tasso is the heart of the town and is a favourite place for meeting friends and for taking a stroll in the evening. The tree-lined square has two statues: the best known is the *Monument to Torquato Tasso*, the poet from Sorrento who was born on the 11th of March 1544 and died in Rome on the April 25th 1595 and is known for his pastoral poem *Aminta* and his epic poem *Jerusalem Freed*. The sculpture was done by G. Carli in 1870. The other statue, which is by Tommaso Solari and dates from 1879, depicts *St. Antony the Abbot* - who is the patron saint of Sorrento and found refuge here during the Longobard invasion - in the act of blessing the town.

Facing onto the square at the beginning of *Corso Italia* is the arcaded **Church of St. Mary del "Carmine"**. Inside the church there is a valuable sanctuary dating from the latter half of the 18th century and an allegoric painting on the ceiling which was carried out by Onofrio Avellino at the beginning of the 18th century.

Sorrento, Tasso Square: the monument to the famous man of letters and a view towards Corso Italia with the façade of the Church of St. Mary "del Carmine".

Sorrento, a sight of the airy tree-lined Tasso Square with the monument to St. Anthony the Abbot carried out by Tommaso Solari in the 19th century.

◀ A view of Sorrento from the port.

Sorrento, the steep rocks tower over the tourist harbour.

THE HARBOUR

Sorrento's long sea front is made up of the *Marina Grande* which is equipped for tourism with its bathing beaches, and the *Marina Piccola*. The latter is the major harbour of the town where the motorboats and hydrofoils which ply the gulf are moored, particularly those going to Naples and the lovely nearby island of Capri. The island which was dear to the great Roman Emperor Tiberius and to a vast number of his contemporary writers, represents an important excursion visit for tourists who find themselves on this fascinating part of the coast, and the Sorrento harbour is an ideal departure point. The harbour also has facilities for the small boats of holidaymakers who arrive here in the summer and is protected by a long jetty.

The sight which greets tourists on their arrival from the sea is delightful. The palaces and buildings cling to the rocky tufa walls which plunge into the deep blue sea, the shimmering colours of which change according to the position of the sun's rays. All along the coast, which is marked by sheer cliffs, are numerous villas and residences with their typically Mediterranean architecture, while the Mediterranean bush and the groves of citrus fruits enhance the lush and sunny landscape.

SEDILE DOMINOVA

This curious name derives from one of the most typical buildings in Sorrento's old town. It is a 15th-century loggia built on a square plan, open on two sides by large rounded Romanesque arches supported on columns which are completed by capitals decorated with flower motifs. The whole is roofed over by a graceful 17th-century dome covered in two-toned majolica which gives the construction an oriental aspect. The "seat" was the expression used by a part of the Sorrento aristocracy who usually met here to discuss matters concerning the town. The interior has architectural decorations, frescoes from the 18th century and numerous coats of arms of the illustrious Sorrento families who belonged to the "seat".

Sorrento, a prospect of the loggia known as Sedile Dominova and detail of its richly decorated interior.

THE CATHEDRAL

Sorrento's Cathedral rose up around the 11th century but was entirely rebuilt in the 15th century on a Renaissance pattern. The modern façade which is inspired by the Gothic style is accompanied by a strange three-storyed campanile topped by a cell which originally was meant to house the bells. The campanile has a clock with a lovely polychrome face and the architecture of the base dates back to Roman times.

The interior is in the form of a Latin cross and the nave is divided into three parts by robust pillars which support rounded arches. Among the many works of art which adorn the interior, which is already richly decorated in marble (some of it dating from Roman and Medieval times) the following are worth special mention: those to be found on the ceiling of the central nave, painted by the Malinconico family: (*Sorrento Martyrs, Four Bishops*); those by Giacomo del Po on the transept ceiling (*The Assumption, St. Philip, St. James*); a valuable 16th-century marble altarpiece; the marble pulpit and the archbishop's throne, both from the 16th century.

Sorrento, the campanile of the Cathedral.

CHURCH AND CLOISTER OF ST. FRANCIS

The 18th-century church dedicated to the saint from Assisi stands in the vicinity of the *Villa Comunale* in a verdant panoramic park shaded by palm trees. Its façade which is on two orders is decorated with pilaster strips. The higher order has a circular window, whilst the curved panel on the summit is topped by a statue. The wooden portal engraved by a 16th-century artist is of great interest.

Next to the church is the convent, the most interesting part of which is the small **Cloister**. This frames the view of the campanile culminating in its characteristic spire and which is in part supported by Roman-age construction work. Two sides of the cloister are broken up by octagonal columns culminating in elegant capitals supporting rounded arches. The other two sides are even more interesting for their intertwining pointed arches, columns and lunettes. This 14th-century portion of the arcade reveals Arab influence.

Sorrento, the Church and the Cloister of St. Francis.

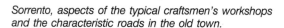

Sorrento, aspects of the typical craftsmen's workshops and the characteristic roads in the old town.

On the following pages: panoramic glimpses towards the Scutari Point and an aspect of the bathing facilities at Sorrento.

ASPECTS OF THE OLD TOWN

As the tourist wanders through the maze of streets in the old town he discovers an unexpected side to Sorrento. The narrow paved streets are flanked by the typical houses with their terraces and balconies. In some parts medieval touches emerge, shown by the type of constructions joined together by slender arches in brick and stone. Along these roads there are characteristic workshops where patient craftsmen display the fruits of their labours, perhaps inviting one inside to make an "excellent bargain".

Elsewhere the inexhaustible inventiveness and estro of this Mediterranean population has led to improvised stalls for a heterogeneous collection of articles, from clothing to handicraft and the unfailing "souvenirs", which are laid out for inspection by the curious tourists.

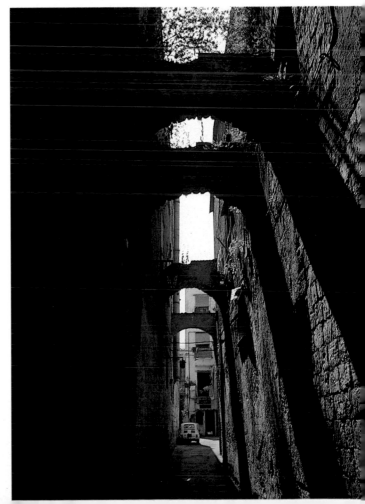

MARINA GRANDE

From the tree-lined *Piazza della Vittoria* (Victory Square), near to which traces of Roman ruins confirm the supposition that there was once a temple to Venus here, one enters the picturesque *Via Marina Grande*. This road connects the old town to the underlying marina and is narrow and tortuous, winding between arches and underpasses by way of ancient buildings and gardens, and terminating in a flight of steps at the pretty port of Marina Grande.

The beaches equipped for bathing with their multi-coloured wooden cabins and colorful sunshades set out on pile structures and leaning against the water-lapped rocks are to be found here. On the sand, around the numerous boats which are drawn up out of the water, the local fishermen mend their nets and hulls. In the centre of this charming cove, framed by the lovely surroundings, are the pleasure boats.

Sorrento: a view of the characteristic countryside which leads to Marina Grande.

Sorrento, a splendid picture of the Marina Grande with the typical bathing facilities and the picturesque fishermen's harbour.

◄ *A Sorrento fisherman repairs his nets.*

Capo di Sorrento, a view of the so-called Queen Joan's Bath.

On the following pages: Capo di Sorrento, remains of the Roman Villa of Pollius Felix; Massa Lubrense, panorama with the Marina della Lobra in the foreground.

BAGNO DELLA REGINA GIOVANNA
(QUEEN JOAN'S BATH)

On arrival at Capo di Sorrento it is a good idea to take an excursion to the evocative Punta del Capo. The trip winds through citrus plantations and olive groves, offering delightful glimpses of the view. On arrival at the extremity of the Point - from where the gaze travels over an extensive view towards the peninsula, the town, the Piano di Sorrento, Punta Gradelle and Mount Faito which plunges into the sea - one can see the remains of a Roman building. It is believed that these (which consist of traces of the foundations, parts of a wall on the landward side, and the remains of walls in *opus reticulatum* and buildings used for bathing in the lower portion towards the sea) were part of the **Villa of Pollius Felix** This belief derives from a particularly good description of the Villa by the Latin poet Publius Papinius Statius (45 - 96 A.D.).

Nearby is the inlet which is known as Queen Joan's Bath, a picturesque crack in the rock allows the sea water to flow into a pool which is transparent and catches the changing light of the sea.

81

Sant'Agata sui due Golfi: panoramic glimpse towards Salerno.

Sant'Agata sui due Golfi: panorama towards the Sorrento plain, the Punta Gradelle and Vesuvius.

MASSA LUBRENSE

This charming holiday town and health resort takes the form of an amphitheatre on the hills above *Marina della Lobra.* The origins of the place name come from a combination of the early Middle Age word *massa* (which was used to indicate a group of rural dwellings and land) and the latin expression *delubrum* (which referred to the presence of an ancient temple, probably dedicated to Minerva).

The **Church of S. Maria delle Grazie** (Our Lady of Grace) is situated in the higher zone of the built-up area. It was renovated in the later part of the 18th century and has a valuable majolic pavement and a painting of *Our Lady of Grace* by Andrea da Salerno.

Marina della Lobra is a picturesque fishing village with well-organized moorings for tourist boats and is the location of the 16th-century **Sanctuary of St. Mary "della Lobra"** which stands on the site occupied by previous places of worship dating back as far as pagan times. It has a majolic floor, a caisson ceiling and a wooden 18th-century *Crucifix*.

SANT'AGATA SUI DUE GOLFI

This pleasant panoramic locality is situated on a high ridge in the lower portion of the peninsula of Sorrento. It is a holiday resort, is well-frequented by tourists, and from here there is an extensive view towards the gulfs of Naples and Sorrento which gives it its name.

The **Church of Our Lady of Grace** is the 17th-century Parish Church and contains 16th- and 17th-century paintings, and a notable main altar which was brought here from a Neapolitan church at the beginning of the last century. This is made out of multi-coloured marble interspersed with semi-precious stones and mother-of-pearl and is the work of 16th-century Florentine artists. The place of major interest to tourists, however, is the **Desert**; originally a Carmelite hermitage which was later used as an orphanage, it is famous for the beautiful sweeping panorama which can be admired from the terrace and which overlooks the two bays, Vesuvius, the Sorrento peninsula and the lovely island of Capri.

CASTELLAMMARE DI STABIA

This largely modern town stands on the south-easterly end of the Parthenopean gulf. Seen from the panoramic road which runs along Mount Faito, one of the highest points of the Lattari mountains which lie to the south of it, it is laid out in a semicircle with the lovely countryside and Vesuvius behind it.

Founded as a Greek colony, it became Etruscan and then Samnite before being Romanized by the name of *Stabiae* in the 4th century B.C. Silla destroyed the town during the civil war in 89 B.C. and the eruption of Vesuvius in 79 A.D. cancelled it from the face of the earth, after which it rose up again as a thermal resort and a castle was built in the 8th century. During both the Middle Ages and modern times it has been repeatedly destroyed.

There is an **Archeological Museum** containing precious remains found during the excavations of the ancient town of Stabiae. The affrescoes, sculptures and basreliefs are of particular interest. In the **Nuove and Antiche Terme Stabiane** (Ancient and Modern Spas) thermal treatment is car-

ried out. These cures were known even to the Romans who found them useful for curing various illnesses. The 16th-century **Cathedral** was restructured by Rispoli at the end of the 19th century. Its interior has a central nave and two aisles and is topped by a high dome. The Cathedral houses frescos from the last century and 6th-century sculpture of *St. Michael*. The 17th-century **Chiesa del Gesù** (Jesus Church) was built for the Jesuits. The spacious interior houses the *Madonna del Soccorso* by Luca Giordano and a *St. Ignatius*, by Paolo de Matteis. Nearby there is the **Villa Comunale**, a green public garden with numerous palm trees giving it an exotic air, several marble busts, and from which there is a splendid view of the gulf framed by Vesuvius. The **Castle** dating from the early Middle Ages was transformed and strengthened during the 12th and 13th centuries. Don't miss a visit to the *archaeological excavations* just outside the town which have uncovered the **Villa Arianna** and a second **Roman Villa**, both rich in decorative features.

Castellammare di Stabia, panoramic vista towards Vesuvius.

A view of Ischia-Porto.

THE ISLAND OF ISCHIA

The largest of the Parthenopean islands is, together with the nearby islands of Procida and Vivara, the result of an intense volcanic activity which overturned the Flegrean Fields region at the beginnings of geological history. The volcanic nature of the island, rather than the structure of its rocks (lava, tufa, magma of trachyte origin) can be deduced by the numerous craters (Montagnone, Mount Rotaro) and by the presence of an ancient volcano (Mount Epomeo), from the volcanic cauldron (the basin forming the port of Ischia) and from the intense thermal activity which together with the characteristic smoke-holes testify to a secondary volcanism which is still active.

The island was colonised in the 7th century B.C. by the Greeks who called it *Phitecusa* and was subsequently inhabited by people from Siracusa and then by the Romans who surrendered it to the Neapolitans in exchange for Capri in the 1st century A.D. It was renamed *Ischia* in the 9th century and came under the Angevins and Aragonese. After suffering repeated Saracene raids during the 16th

and 17th centuries it passed to the Bourbons and took part in the national unification of 1861. The island has undergone frequent natural turmoils during its millenial history; from the eruptions which forced the Siracusans to flee (6th to 5th centuries B.C.), to that of 1302, including the ruinous earthquakes which have so often tried the tenacity and willpower of its population. The tremor which completely destroyed the village of Casamicciola on the 28th of July 1883 is tragically famous.

Ischia has been rightly named the "Emerald Island" because of its naturally lush Mediterranean vegetation and for the presence of plants which are more usually found in warmer climates. The mild climate of Ischia, the excellent quality of its vines (which produce the well-known Epomeo white wine) and olives, and the citrus groves make this island a small paradise. It has always been known for its thermal springs and has well-equipped modern hotels and baths which cater for treatments.

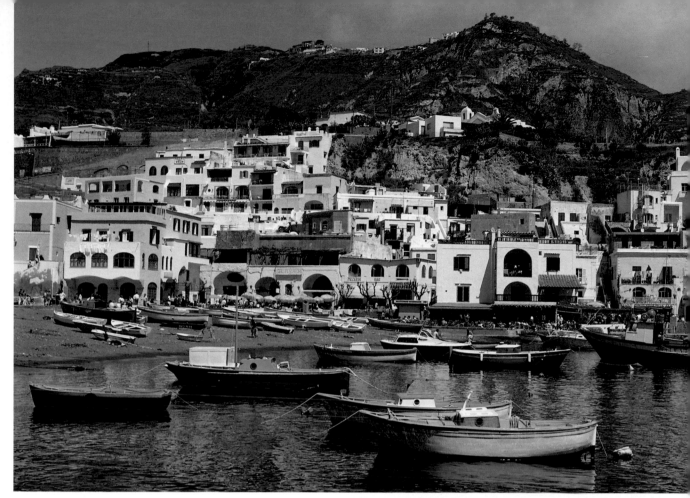

◄ *Panorama of Ischia from the Aragonese castle.*

Sant'Angelo d'Ischia, an evocative view of the houses overlooking the picturesque Arenile.

Forío d'Ischia, a lovely picture of the marina.

FORÍO

On the western slopes of Mount Epomeo overlooking Punta del Soccorso is one of the most picturesque localities on the island. Its territory has been inhabited since remote times but it was above all the Romans who appreciated the health-giving thermal waters and its exceptional geographical position. In ancient times the huge *Citara* beach which Punta del Soccorso divides from *Chiaia* was consecrated to the worship of Venus and Apollo. During the early Middle Ages and at the beginning of modern times its coast, which is one of the most exposed on the island, was reinforced by numerous watch-towers in order to keep the pirate fleets under control. The most noted of these towers is the robust 15th-century circular **Tower** which still dominates the picturesque harbour. Also worth mentioning are the 18th-19th century **Parish Church of St. Vito**, the 14th-century **Church of St. Mary of Loreto** and the **"Soccorso" Chapel**.

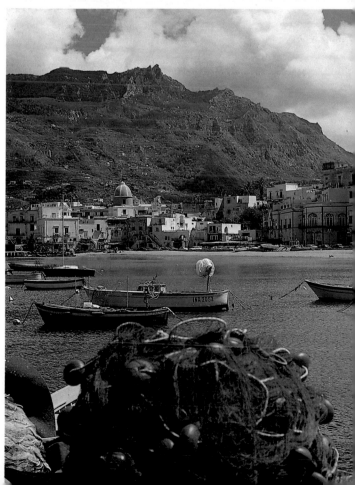

◀ *A picturesque glimpse of Ischia-Ponte.*

Forío d'Ischia, an angle of the characteristic harbour with the 15th-century tower.

SANT'ANGELO D'ISCHIA

Sant'Angelo d'Ischia is a delightful holiday resort, excellently equipped for sea-bathing and thermal treatment and is rightly considered one of the gems of the "Emerald Island". It occupies a lovely position at the edge of the *Arenile dei Maronti* (Maronti Beach) on the southern coast between Mount Epomeo and the trachyte peninsula of Sant'Angelo, and is a perfect spot in which to forget the pace and stress of modern times. The ruined *tower* is a reminder of the old battles between the English and the French. The small jetty is enlivened by the colourful fishing boats and overlooked by the brilliant white houses of the fishing village, while the arches, open terraces and loggias enhance the charm.

The beautiful **Maronti Lido** testifies to the volcanic nature of the island, with its numerous thermal springs and smoke-holes.

◄ *View of Ischia with the island of Procida in the background.*

◄ *Ischia, picturesque aspect of the seaside village.*

Ischia, a picture of the Castle and the Spanish Aqueduct.

ISCHIA

The island's main port and calling-point for the ferries and hydrofoil boats which link it to the mainland faces onto the channel which separates the "Emerald Island" from Procida. The pleasant tourist haunt is endowed with a well-organized thermal structure. The locality, which is also a seaside resort, is singular because of the bipolar structure of its urban core.

The picturesque quarter **Ischia Ponte** is situated to the south, joined by the so-called *Aragonese Bridge* (15th century) to the round trachyte island on which stand the massive walls which encircle **Ischia Castle**, a fortification which was erected in subsequent eras.

To the north is the **Ischia Porto** quarter which is more modern and which grew up around the cauldron of an ancient volcano and was subsequently transformed into a harbour. Among other notable features we would point out the 19th-century **Terme Comunale** (Communale Baths); the 14th-century **Cathedral of the Assumption** later restructured in Baroque style, and the neoclassic **Church of St. Mary of Porto Salvo** (late 19th century).

Sant'Angelo d'Ischia, prospect of the Aphrodite's Spa and the romantic Maronti Lido.

Lacco Ameno: the "Fungo" ("Mushroom"). ►

Forío d'Ischia, Sanctuary of St. Maria del Soccorso. ►

ASPECTS OF THE ISLAND

The variety of Ischia, its fascinating and changeable countryside, its singular and generous nature, the ancient thermal cures and the typical nature of some of its buildings, can only be understood by being seen. This is certainly the case of the **Aphrodite's Spa** one of the thermal resorts on Ischia, which is situated in the idyllic scenery of the *Maronti Lido*. An elegant thermal-water swimming pool shaded by palms and overlooking the magical view of the sea renders the idea of the way the island has been adapted to tourism. The evocative **Fungo** (Mushroom) at Lacco Ameno, whose very name calls up a picture of the beauty and magic of the locality, is one of the best-known sights on the riviera. The **Sanctuary-Chapel of St. Mary "del Soccorso"** at Forio is an example of island architecture and popular religiousness. Inside the candid building which stands to great effect on a panoramic terrace, there are the ex-voto of sailors, a painting of *St. Augustine* and a *Crucifixion*, which according to local tradition was found after a storm.

◄ *A view of the picturesque town of Procida.*

Procida, glimpse of the characteristic old town.

THE ISLAND OF PROCIDA

The lesser of the Flegrean Islands is separated from Capo Miseno by the Channel of Procida and is close to Ischia. Together with the latter and the small island of Vivara, Procida is one of the best morphological examples of volcanic activity in the Flegrean Fields' region. That Procida is the result of undersea eruptions, like the rest of the Flegrean area, is proved by the composition of its rocks which include tufa and trachyte, but also some basalt. The irregular outline of the Procida coast also proves its volcanic origins, revealing the rims of at least five craters.

The island was already inhabited in prehistoric times and was colonised by the Greeks who named it *Próchyta*. Up until the end of the 18th century the island shared the fortunes of nearby Ischia, being repeatedly occupied by the English during their struggles with the French. In the 13th century it belonged to the noble Da Procida family, from whom it took its present name and whose descendent Giovanni is the most famous of its members.

The island is full of picturesque features: from the splendid beaches looking out over the blue sea to the romantic Points of Solchiato and Pioppeto where delightful views are to be had, and including the island's characteristic town centre. The town of Procida has colourfully painted houses which lend it a typically Mediterranean air, and its architecture is rendered almost oriental by the use of arches. The terraces, domes, narrow alleys and underpasses combine to make Procida unique. One of the most interesting parts is the ancient village of *Terra Murata* with its **Church of St. Michael** which was originally part of an abbey and has a caisson ceiling with a painting by Luca Giordano representing *St. Michael destroying Lucifer* (17th century). Not far from the *Marina di Sancio Cattolico*, the main landing-place on Procida, is the **Sanctuary of Our Lady of Grace**. The building is topped by a high dome resting on a polygonal tambour; inside are the resting places of the 12 Procidian martyrs (1799).

Pozzuoli, two lovely pictures of the so-called Temple of Serapis, actually a Roman - age public marketplace.

POZZUOLI

This large town stands on the central portion of the gulf of the same name in a most evocative position, and is delimited by Miseno and the island of Nisida. It is a much-frequented spa and sea-side resort with an active industrial and commercial sector. It is the main port of call for boats to the Flegrean Islands, and is also a centre of great archaeological, geological and artistic interest. Its position in the Flegrean Fields, in an area which is still subject to volcanic activity, means that its territory is conditioned by centuries-old bradyseismic movements and recurring telluric events.

It became a colony of Samos in the second part of the 6th century B.C. Previously it had been known as *Dikaiarchia* and had fought beside Cumae against the Etruscans and the Samnites, who conquered it in the second part of the 5th century B.C. In the 2nd century B.C. under the Romans it took the name of *Puteoli*, becoming well-known as a port and probably becoming the main strategic base for the Roman fleet in the Mediterranean until the foundation of the port of Ostia (1st century A.D.). In spite of its decline at this period, it was held in great esteem by the Emperors and particularly by Domitian who connected it to the capital by a road which took his name. St. Paul visited it and mentioned it in his ''Acts of the Apostles'', and it suffered repeated Barbarian invasions after the fall of the Roman Empire (5th - 6th centuries A.D.). These invasions coupled with the intense bradyseismic activity drove the population to Naples and other places which were considered safer. At the same time the gradual submersion of the original port structure turned the locality into a fishing centre, adding incentive to the activities connected with the natural spas. In more recent times the increase of bradyseism and geological unsettlement has determined the evacuation of some parts of the old town, throwing into relief in an alarming way the precariousness of the Flegrean territory.

Pozzuoli, some pictures of the conspicuous remains of the Flavian Amphitheatre.

THE TEMPLE OF SERAPIS

This is one of the major monumental testimonies to the Roman Age, also known as *Serapeo*, and reveals traces of a *jetty* from the Augustinian era. Although its name comes from the discovery of a statue to *Serapis*, an ancient Egyptian divinity worshipped during the Greek and Roman eras, the massive structure which we can see today was a public marketplace of considerable dimensions. The *Macellum*, originally destined for the sale of foodstuffs, and in particular meat and fish, occupied a four-sided space enclosed by collonades onto which opened the shops which were also accessible from the outside. On the side opposite the main entrance there was a semicircular room containing several niches with statues. The central portion of the courtyard was occupied by a circular podium with a central fountain which was decorated with statues. A group of 16 columns in African marble, culminating in Corinthian capitals held up the trabeation on which rested, originally, a dome. This construction dates back to the

Flavian period, but various conservation works were carried out after an earthquake during the 1st century A.D. and in later periods (2nd-3rd centuries A.D.). The temple of Serapis is of great interest to us today, apart from its exceptional architectural and archaeological value, because it enables us to "read" at a glance the dynamics of centuries of bradyseism at Pozzuoli. The ruins are partially submerged in the seawater and in thermal-mineral water which has seeped in as a result of the sinking ground level. On the remains of the columns which rise from the central podium and on the three large columns which remain standing of the four which once stood in front of the semicircular room opening onto the collonade, one can see the holes produced by the litodomi - a type of mollusc which bores into the stone onto which it clings - and enables us to visibly verify the progressive rise and fall of the water level as a consequence of bradyseism.

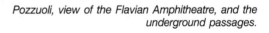

Pozzuoli, view of the Flavian Amphitheatre, and the underground passages.

FLAVIAN AMPHITHEATRE

In the upper part of the town, in an area which contains other Roman ruins such as the *Small Amphitheatre* (where lie the ruins in *opus incertum* of a construction built during the reign of Augustus) and the *Piscina Cardito* (a system of communicating cisterns) stand the imposing ruins of the Flavian Amphitheatre. It was completed during the reign of the Emperor Titus Flavius Vespasian in the second half of the 1st century A.D. and is in fact, in chronological order, much older than the Small Amphitheatre. As regards size, it is the third largest amphitheatre of Classical times coming after the Colosseum (Rome) and the amphitheatre at Santa Maria Capua Vetere. This remarkable work, which gives testimony to the skill of the Roman builders, is still in an excellent state of conservation, due largely to the presence of layer upon layer of volcanic deposits and scoriae, which have gradually built up over the centuries because of the eruptions of the nearby Solfatara. The first archaeological finds were brought to light after archaeological digs were carried out in the first half of the last century. After having been concealed for years

Pozzuoli, some images of the fascinating underground passages at the Flavian Amphitheatre.

under an enormous accumulation of volcanic deposits, it was finally restored to its former grandeur in the late 1940's. The surrounding edifice of the amphitheatre originally had three orders of arcades, with a crowning wall. The interior has the form of an ellipse and measures 75 m by 42 m; it is divided trasversely by a corridor covered with grilles as are the numerous trapdoors set in the ground-floor wall of the arena which were used during the performances. Originally, the cavea (horseshoe shaped auditorium) had three tiers of seats, although only two tiers, which are, on the whole, well preserved, can be seen today. The amphitheatre had a seating capacity of 40.000; a series of steps led to the various sections of the tiers and these flights of steps divided the auditorium into wedgeshaped sections which can still be made out today. The spectators reached the tiers by means of the vomitoria (an entrance way through which the spectators passed in order to reach their seats) and these can also be seen today.

But the most interesting architectural feature of the building, which conjures up images of the games and performances which took place in the amphitheatre, is the network of **Underground Passages**. These take the form of corridors which ran under the ellipse and have the same oval form as the latter and there are also two corridors which intersect each other at right angles. These underground passages, built for the greater part of brick, were completed during the 1st and 2nd centuries A.D. and are stil well preserved today. These provide us with clear visible evidence of the circus games and, more particularly, the contests fought out between the gladiators and the ferocious animals. Today we know for certain that the numerous trap-doors set into the ground floor wall of the arena were opened by a complex system of ropes and pulleys, thereby releasing the wild animals into the arena. These openings, which provide ventilation for the underground passages, were also the means by which scenery and props used in the performance were brought into the arena. It has also been proved that by means of a hydraulic mechanism, water was drawn from a nearby aqueduct in the Campana region and the water obtained was used to flood the arena so that the performances of naval battles (known as *Naumachie*) could be put on. After restructuring work carried out in a section of the underground passages in the second half of the 17th century, the **Chapel of St. Januarius** was built in keeping with the age-old tradition according to which, the future patron saint of Naples, together with his followers, is said to have been thrown to the animals, who, however, left the saint completely unharmed.

Pozzuoli, the desolate scene of the Solfatara.

SOLFATARA

Just outside the town, a road leading off the *Via Domiziana* leads to Solfatara, one of the few remaining volcanic formations to be seen today in the area known as the Flegrean Fields. It was known in Roman times as *Forum Vulcani*, and is in fact the large crater of a dormant volcano. The dormant period of this volcanic formation near Pozzuoli (which is known as "di solfatara"-literally "of solfatara") is one of the typical stages of post-volcanic activity; a period when the only sign of life of a dormant volcano is when it produces sulphureous gases which, when they condense, create sulphur deposits.

However, a visit to Solfatara, which should only be undertaken in the company of an expert or guide is an extremely interesting experience. The desolate and deserted countryside has an almost unreal feel to it, and the only tangible signs on the landscape are the emission of steam at high temperatures (around 100°C), hot mud springs (also known as *little volcanoes of mud*), the release of carbon dioxide into the air (*mofettes*) and mineral water springs. The volcano last erupted at the turn of the 12th century. The crater itself has an elliptical shape, whilst its walls are made up of tufaceous and trachytic rocks. The only buildings to be seen inside the crater are the ancient *Observatory*, situated close to the so-called *Bocca Grande* (the *Large Mouth* of the crater) and the *Furnaces*, from which steam which reaches temperatures of around 100°C is let off. One of the most characteristic phenomenon which can be seen inside the crater of Solfatara is the condensation of water vapour which forms little clouds in the presence of a naked flame.

Pozzuoli, some scenes of the Solfatara and its volcanic manifestations.

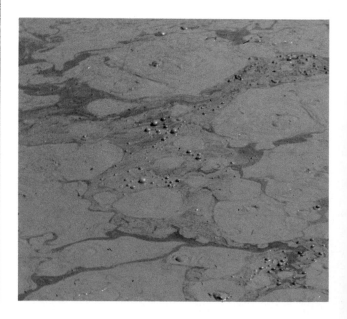

Panorama of Bacoli and Capo Miseno, in the background the characteristic profile of Capri can be seen.

A prospect of the Castle of Baia and the ample panorama which is seen from Miseno.

BACOLI-CAPO MISENO

For those who approach Bacoli by means of the picturesque road which dominates the western part of the Gulf of Pozzuoli, Bacoli is heralded by the imposing square-shaped structure known as **Baia Castle**. This was built on the orders of Don Pedro di Toledo, the viceroy of Spain, in the 16th century in order to protect the riverside locality from the incessant pirate raids to which it was subjected at that time. Bacoli is a town with an important fishing industry and is also a well-known seaside resort. The ancient centre of the town, founded by the Greeks, was a favourite spot with the Romans, who built sumptuous villas and residences here. There are numerous remains of the Roman *Bauli* still to be seen today. The **Cento Camerelle** (meaning literally a hundred small chambers), a two-storeyed water reservoir, is a complex system which provides water to one of the nearby villas of the district. The most ancient part is that of the lower section and is made up of a network of underground passages which run down to the sea. In the upper section stands an enormous cistern which dates back to the 1st century A.D. The socalled **Piscina Mirabile** is a large Roman cistern which was used by the Roman fleet moored near the Capo Miseno. This is believed to be the largest cistern of ancient times and was built during the reign of Augustus. Near the beach stand the ruins of what is mistakenly known as the **Tomb of Agrippina**. However these ruins have nothing to do with the mother of Nero, who, on her son's orders was killed and buried at Bauli. They are infact the visible remains of a little theatre connected to a large Roman villa which looks out over the sea.

The Capo Miseno, which is all that remains of an ancient volcano which slopes down towards the sea, dominates a unique landscape which is marked by numerous volcanic craters (Lake Miseno and the Port of Miseno) and gives visible evidence of the volcanic nature of this seaside territory of the Flegrean Fields. In shape, it is reminiscent of the tumulus tombs and maybe this fact perpetuates the myth that the Cape was the site of the burial grounds of mythical persons and characters. Its slopes are dotted with Roman ruins, amongst which mention should be made of the ruins of the villa of Caius Marius. In the Augustan Age, the port of Miseno became the most important seat of the Roman military fleet which dropped anchor in the Tyrrhenian Sea. It is probably due to this fact that the present day fishing village bearing the same name came into existance.

Archaeological zone of Baia: two pictures of the Nymphaeum-Theatre with its circular basin.

BAIA

The locality, which forms part of the Commune of Bacoli, is a seaside village and a well-known bathing resort which stretches out picturesquely along the gulf from which its name is derived. However the locality is famous above all for the fact that a vast archaeological zone is situated here; in this the westernmost part of the Gulf of Naples remarkable ruins that date back to the Roman times have been found.

The Roman town of *Baiae* began to flourish from the time of the Late Republican Age. During this period, the natural abundance of its thermal waters together with a pleasant and inviting climate led the Romans to build many splendid residences and elegant villas for the Roman aristocracy amidst the enchanting landscape of the picturesque bay of Baia, which has been celebrated in verse by the poets and writers of the Latinity. If the citations of Horace, Titus, Livy, Martial and Statius alone suffice to sing the praises of the locality, the villas belonging to prominent members of the Roman political and social scene which were built here are testimony to the considerable residential calling of Baia, the likes of which it would be difficult to find elsewhere. During the Imperial Age the territory became the exclusive residence of the Emperors who bought up the private residences thus bestowing an air of grandeur to a locality which, on a par with Capri, entered into the limited number of Imperial "gems". Baia thus became the stage on which several episodes of the tormented story of Rome under the Caesars were carried out, including crimes and heedlessness but also ambitious projects and displays of mad eccentricity.

Later in its history the headlong progression of profound sinking caused by bradyseism together with the disastrous effects of the repeated eruptions of the Flegrean volcanoes, caused the almost total disappearance of the Roman settlement and of the splendid testimonies to its grandeur. Only after the Second World War were excavations begun in order to bring to the surface some of the conspicuous remains of the Roman town.

Archeological zone of Baia: some pictures of buildings and rooms probably used as a Spa.

ARCHEOLOGICAL ZONE

Along a terraced slope which begins at the top of the hill are the imposing remains of the ancient Imperial *Palatium* which was only in part destined to be used as a Spa. The date of these buildings is from the 1st to the 4th century A.D.; the ruins, joined to each other by ramps, staircases and corridoors, are divided into sectors - *Sosandra, Mercury and Venus*. **Sosandra's Sector**, so-named because of a marble bust from that period (copied from an original Greek bronze in the 5th century B.C.) which was found in an internal room, displays the remains of a residence and a *Nymphaeum-Theatre* with a circular basin. A wide lower terrace holds the remains of the so-called *Sosandra's Bath*, a porticoed pool the waters of which were supplied by a thermal source which is still active. **Mercury's Sector**,

Baia, the Temple of Venus.

Baia, the ruins of the Temple of Diana.

wrongly believed to have been a temple, is a circular building whose walls, *in opus reticulatum* held up the hemispherical vault. It was almost certainly used as a thermal installation. The **Venus's Sector**, set on different levels of the terraces, was made up of various rooms one of which held the *Esedra-Nymphaeum* which contained a fountain. The rest of the archaeological remains of Baia consist of the Temples of Venus and Diana. The **Temple of Venus**, in all probability once connected to the sector of the same name, seen from the outside has an octagonal shape with large windows. The entrance is flanked by niches and there are others around the external perimeter of the building. The inside, which is on a circular plan, is open to the sky since the vault which originally covered it has been destroyed. Outside the actual archaeological zone, not far from the Cumae railway station, is the **Temple of Diana**. This building has structural and architectural similiarities to the Temple of Venus, whose plan and shape it resembles. The roof which once covered it is only partially conserved and this contributes to giving the building a strange architectural aspect.

Cumae, view of Apollo's Temple.

On the following pages: Cumae, view of Apollo's Temple and details of the Via Sacra.

CUMAE

The archaeological zone of Cumae is among the most interesting in the area and stretches to the south of the reclaimed plain of Licola on the high ground between the Tyrrhenian Sea and the Averno lake. One of the most progressive Greek settlements in southern Italy grew up here, when Chaldean settlers from Euboea settled here in the 8th century B.C., on the place already occupied during Prehistoric times and which, according to historical sources, was previously elected headquarters by colonists arriving from Aeolia as far back as the 11th century B.C. The power of the State of Cumae grew rapidly and soon brought the surrounding region, from Miseno to *Puteoli*, into submission thus creating the basis for the foundation of *Neapolis*. Plotted against by the Etruscans and other Italic populations who were envious of its power, Cumae won decisive victories in the 6th and 5th centuries B.C., the last of which brought about the final fall of the Etruscan expansion in Magna Grecia. However, after being brought into submission by the Samnites in the second part of the 5th century B.C. and successively falling under the Romans, it gave a positive help to the nearby powerful city at the time of the Punic Wars, consequently becoming a *Municipium*. It declined during the Early Middle Ages and was razed to the ground by Saracene pirates in the 10th century after which it suffered an irreversible disintegration.

Cumae, panorama towards the Spa and the Temple of the Capitoline Triad.

Cumae, two view of Jupiter's Temple. ►

ARCHAEOLOGICAL ZONE

The archaeological site at Cumae, which is made up of the numerous remains of temples, public and private buildings, the Acropolis and a vast cemetery, is situated between the pine woods at Licola and the so-called **Arco Felice**, which stands guard over the entrance to this interesting testimony of past ages. The arch is formed from a single barrel-vault and was raised in the 1st century A.D., at the time of Domitian. Nearby is the so-called *Grotta di Cocceio* (The Grotto of Cocceius) which is actually an underground passage which joins the town to the Averno lake. Further along, the road branches off: One branch leads to the scarce traces of the **Amphitheatre** (1st century B.C.) while the other one leads to the huge **Necropolis**

where traces of Roman burial sites from the Republican and Imperial eras have been uncovered, and also ancient tombs dating from between the 9th and 7th centuries B.C. which present similarities to Mycenaean funeral architecture.

After passing the so-called *Sybil's Cave* one arrives at the zone of the *Forum*. The wide area, in part arcaded, held the Temple of the Capitoline Triad and the **Spa**, built between the 1st and the 2nd centuries A.D. The **Temple of the Capitoline Triad** which dates from the 4th century B.C. was transformed in the Imperial age. The building has yielded a considerable amount of fragments of the sculptures of the gods which once decorated it. The *Acropolis*

◄ *Cumae, Jupiter's Temple (baptismal font) and the Acropolis.*

Cumae, the archaeological zone in the vicinity of the Cave of the Cumaean Sibyl.

On the following pages: Cumae, two pictures of the Cave of the Sibyl.

presents clear traces of the Greek fortifications (5th century B.C.), on which were superimposed Roman buildings, and which were destined to improve the defences of a position which was already almost inacessible, given the asperity of the location. The Acropolis is reached by the *Via Sacra* a road which was constructed using wide slabs of volcanic rock. On the right are the ruins of **Apollo's Temple**, a Greek building reconstructed in the Samnite and Roman eras. It was originally a peripteral building and the remains of columns and foundations dating back to alterations made during the Augustan period can be seen. Between the 6th and 7th centuries the Temple was reconverted to a Christian Basilica. Also dating from that period there are some tombs and the baptismal font.

At the summit of the Acropolis area, on a spot from where one can admire an extensive panorama, is the **Jupiter's Temple** which is similar in structure to that of Apollo. Its origins are Greek (5th century B.C.), but it was completely reconstructed under Augustus, making it impossible to identify the original portion of the building.

This was also reconverted to a Christian Basilica during the 5th-6th centuries, and there are well-preserved remains of a baptismal font, pieces of wall in *opus reticulatum* and the remains of Christian burial-places. One of the most famous features of the archaeological zone at Cumae is the **Cave of the Cumaean Sibyl**. This was one of the most frequently-visited sanctuaries of the ancient world and was dug out of the tufa rock by the Greeks (6th - 5th century B.C.) to form a quadrilateral section which proceeds into the rock face for about 100 metres. It is fairly well conserved, apart from the initial part which is uncovered, and shows signs of later changes (4th - 3rd centuries B.C.). There is a marble epigraph with verses from Virgil's "Aeneas", some cisterns and a rectangular room with a niche which is considered the place where the Sibyl uttered her prophecies. Not far from the tunnel is the entrance to the so-called *Roman Crypt*, a huge cavity dug into the Cumaean mountainside whose funtion is presumed to have been related to the grotto of Cocceius.

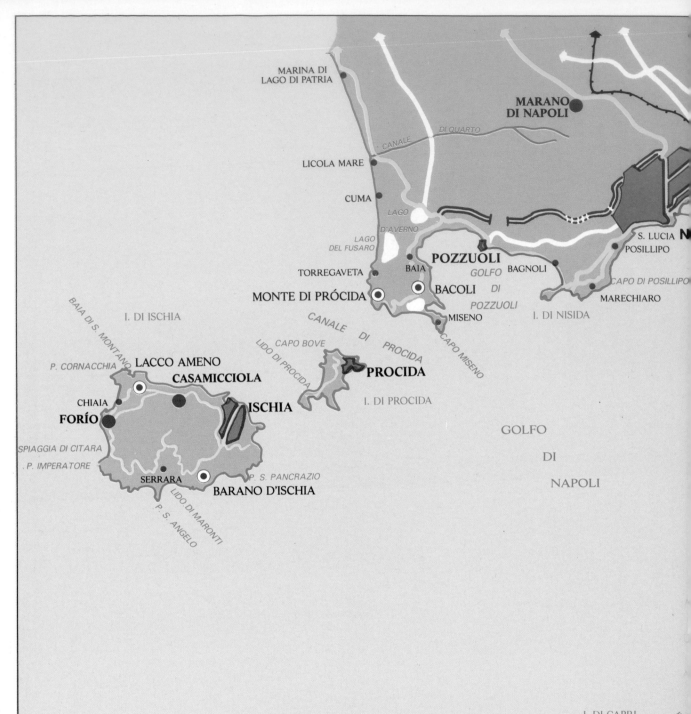

MARINA DI
LAGO DI PATRIA

MARANO
DI NAPOLI

CANALE   DI QUARTO

LICOLA MARE

CUMA

LAGO
D'AVERNO

LAGO
DEL FUSARO

POZZUOLI

S. LUCIA   N

POSILLIPO

TORREGAVETA

BAIA

BAGNOLI

GOLFO

CAPO DI POSILLIPO

MONTE DI PRÓCIDA

BACOLI

DI

MARECHIARO

I. DI ISCHIA

BAIA DI S. MONTANO

CANALE   DI   PROCIDA

POZZUOLI

MISENO

CAPO MISENO

I. DI NISIDA

CAPO BOVE

LIDO DI PROCIDA

PROCIDA

P. CORNACCHIA

LACCO AMENO

CASAMICCIOLA

I. DI PROCIDA

GOLFO

CHIAIA

ISCHIA

DI

FORÍO

SPIAGGIA DI CITARA

NAPOLI

. P. IMPERATORE

SERRARA

P. S. PANCRAZIO

LIDO DI MARONTI

BARANO D'ISCHIA

P. S. ANGELO

I. DI CAPRI

IL C

VILLA S. MICHELE

GROTTA AZZURRA

MAR

ANACAPRI

MARI

CA

P. CARENA

GROTTA VERDE

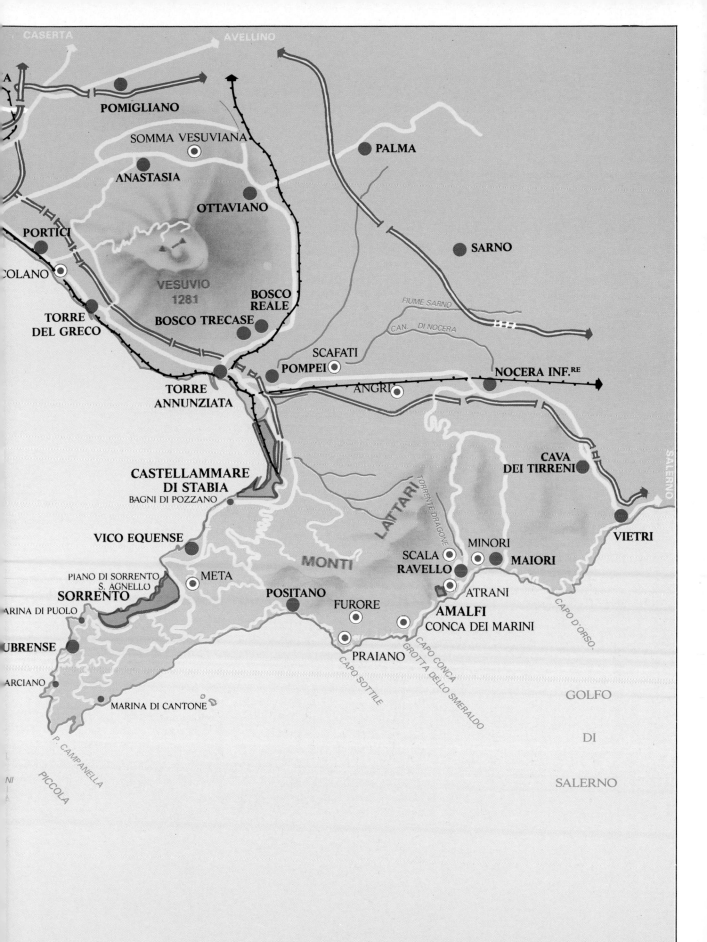

CONTENTS